legacy love letters

HOW TO LEAVE A LEGACY
GIFT OF LOVE, FAITH, HOPE,
AND GRATITUDE

GWEN CHRISTESON

Published by hope*books
2217 Matthews Township Pkwy
Suite D302
Matthews, NC 28105
www.hopebooks.com

hope*books is a division of hope*media

Printed in the United States of America

First paperback edition.
Paperback ISBN: 979-8-89185-286-0
Hardcover ISBN: 979-8-89185-288-4
Ebook ISBN: 979-8-89185-289-1
Library of Congress Number: 2025943231

hb
hope*books

Endorsements

"Legacy love letters will help you write and share your story, so your loved ones avoid some of the pain you've had to walk through. Gwendolyn shows you how your letters can express hope and encouragement for a lasting impact."

– Brian Dixon,
Founder hope*books & Author

"Many attorneys know how to produce trusts, wills, and other legal documents that express the wishes of people engaged in estate planning. But most critical to the process, Gwen has captured the 'why' of estate planning. It is not just about avoiding probate and deciding who gets what. It is about expressing our heartfelt love for family, passion for certain charities, and expression of our deepest hope for those we leave behind. With Gwen's guidance, we can comfort those who grieve our passing and encourage them to become all that God intended them to be."

– Stephen Lindsey,
Founder Lindsey Enterprises,
Inc. & Author of *Wrestling Along The Way: A Journey In Christian Faith*

"When my mom passed away, I discovered a letter she had written to me. In the midst of heartbreak, her words brought an unexpected peace. That letter became a sacred part of my grieving process—her voice, her love, her presence captured in ink. It was the most meaningful gift she could have left behind.

That's why Legacy Love Letters by Gwen Christeson is such an important book. Gwen gently guides you through the process of writing a letter to those you love most—something they can hold onto long after you're gone. Her wisdom and compassion shine through every page, helping you craft a legacy that goes beyond possessions or estate plans.

Having experienced firsthand how powerful one letter can be, I believe this book is a beautiful, healing invitation—for both the writer and the reader. It's a must read for anyone who wants to make sure to leave nothing unsaid to the most important people in their lives."

– Anne Watson,
Host of The Girlfriends
Guide to an Empty Nest podcast

"I had the privilege of sitting next to Gwen at the HopeStory 2024 conference when Legacy Love Letters was still just a seed of a dream—and now here it is, fully blooming. This book is more than a project—it's a sacred invitation to pass on the things that last: love, faith, and gratitude. With the heart of a guide and the wisdom of experience, Gwen helps you write words that will outlive you—words that bless, anchor, and speak life long after you're gone. Legacy Love Letters is a gift for anyone who longs to leave a legacy that truly matters."

– Molinda (Mo) Hern,
Host of the I Choose Today Podcast

This book is dedicated with love to:

my husband Erik,
my son Connor,
my daughters Kate and Brynn,
my grandson Dean, and
my daughter-in-law Madison,
with gratitude to:
my friend and mentor Lynn Hart Muto
who not only introduced me to the field of estate planning
but showed me by example how to
act justly, love mercy, and to walk humbly with God.

Acknowledgments

To Everyone who shared their letters and impact stories, I thank you with a full heart of gratitude for helping me with my passion project and this publication.

To Anne Watson, I thank you for letting God use you to speak truth into my life and career goals. I hired you as a business strategy coach but in return found a lifelong friend and a sister in Christ. You were the first person who told me, "You should write a book." In fact, you were the brave one who, after seeing the first outline, told me you would not buy a book written by an attorney about estate planning. Your honesty forced me to write the legacy book God wanted me to write. Your recommendation to go to the 2024 hope*writers conference helped me find my author community and my publisher.

To Brian Dixon and hope*books, I thank you and your team for helping me embrace my calling as a published Christian author. May your coaching and publishing company bless authors and readers for years to come.

To Molinda (Mo) Hern, I am thankful that we met at the 2024 hope*story conference. By sharing your hard story, you encouraged me to recognize God wanted to draw close to me during my grief journey. May your online community and your podcast continue to bless your listeners for years to come.

Table of Contents

Foreword

This book made me who I am today.

Not in the sense that I somehow managed to get my hands on an early and unreleased manuscript and studied its words and principles throughout my childhood; but in the sense that its author, my mother Gwen Christeson, has been imparting on me the contents of this book my entire life.

Legacy Love Letters is a written account of Gwen's passion for leaving a legacy of love in all facets of her life: as a Christian, as a mother and wife, as a community member, and as a friend. This book isn't just a step-by-step guide on how to make sure your loved ones are comforted in their grief when you pass; but it is a lifelong mission that Gwen has been living and now shares with you, the reader. When you craft your legacy love letter, your life story and wisdom are preserved for future generations, whether they need to hear your voice in good times or bad.

Gwen invites and encourages you to leave behind something that material possessions cannot impart. Her work allows you to bestow upon your loved ones the treasures of your heart. Through tools, inspiration, and heartwarming stories, Gwen guides you through the difficult and emotional process of thinking through what you will leave behind, what your legacy will be. The contents of this book embody the love and principles that I am so grateful to have been given by my mother, Gwen Christeson.

Sincerely, Connor J. Christeson

Prayer for legacy love letters

Dear God,

We praise you for creating Heaven and Earth and all of mankind; your marvelous creation is a work of art.

Your wondrous works are to be remembered, an inheritance is to be handed down from one generation to the next.

You are the author of our legacy story, which is written as we live fully in pursuit of a deeper faith and a more meaningful life.

A legacy life that glorifies you is one captivated with purpose as we store our treasures in Heaven, since our earthly life does not consist in the abundance of possessions.

Your legacy gifts are irrevocable; you gifted each one of us the unique personalities and talents to qualify us to do the life's work you created us to do.

Thank you for creating each one of us to live the extraordinary life and legacy you designed for us to glorify you. Thank you for opening our eyes to what truly matters: to love, know, obey and serve you.

Your legacy plan for each one of us is to use the gifts of time, talent, and treasure you have given us to love the people around us by demonstrating your love in words and actions.

Help us recognize the brevity of life so we don't intentionally disregard a sense of urgency and miss the opportunity to write legacy love letters to help our loved ones grieve differently.

We pray for our loved ones during their time of grief, and we thank you our last words will give them love and eternal hope upon our passing and help them grieve with peace, joy and the hope of Heaven.

Thank you for inviting our loved ones to turn toward you and find comfort and healing until we are reunited in Heaven.

You have victory over the power of death, and you will faithfully fulfill your promise that our reward for this legacy life will be to see you one day.

Until then, may we glorify you as we use the gifts and calling you gave us to love and serve the people in our lives as we use the time we have left to be Awake, to be Real, and to Speak Truth.

In Jesus' name, Amen.

PART ONE

WHY LEGACY MATTERS: HIS WONDROUS WORKS TO BE REMEMBERED

"He has caused his wondrous works to be remembered; the Lord is gracious and merciful."
–Psalm 111:4, ESV

Introduction: *Author's Welcome Letter*

Dear Readers,

Hello and Welcome to Legacy Love Letters!

I am writing you this letter because I care about you, and I care about your legacy. I want to inspire you to see your life and legacy the way God sees it because He cares about you, and He cares about your legacy, too. My book is divided into three parts to answer your questions on why legacy matters; what legacy matters; and how to leave a lasting legacy.

I want you to know about legacy love letters before it is too late. A legacy love letter is a heartfelt final goodbye, which is found and read after the passing of a loved one. A legacy love letter is more than an ordinary love letter because it has an everlasting impact, and it will be treasured long after you're gone. You have the chance to remind your loved ones your final goodbye is only temporary, since you will be reunited with them in Heaven someday. When you leave a legacy love letter, your legacy gift of love, faith, hope, and gratitude will help your loved ones grieve differently. Instead of grieving like the rest of men who have no hope, your loved ones will grieve with the hope of Heaven which will fill their hearts with peace and joy.

I have always had a heart for legacy; God created me that way. I have run a successful law center for over two decades helping clients with estate planning, probate, and trust administration. My legal services give clients peace of mind as I help them put their legal affairs in order. Through my experiences as a licensed California probate attorney, I discovered the most important part of an estate plan is a legacy love letter. A will and trust can only provide an inheritance of earthly treasures, houses, money and personal belongings to loved ones. While working with grieving family members, I learned firsthand their memories of their lost loved ones and the legacy gift of love, faith, hope, and gratitude were much more important than all the stuff left behind. This is why I want to teach you how to take important steps during your lifetime to leave a legacy: a love letter ensures you will be remembered and your loved ones won't be left empty-handed at the time they need love and comfort the most.

Not only did God create me with a heart for legacy, He wrote a message on my heart to inspire and encourage people to write legacy love letters. This passion led me to write this hope*book to reach as many people as I can with this important message: to teach readers about legacy love letters and how they can leave a meaningful legacy gift for those left behind. My mission is to help people prioritize and complete the important legacy gift only they can write. Those who write legacy love letters leave an extraordinary legacy that glorifies God. Their letters have an everlasting impact as they share their Christian faith and remind their loved ones they will see them again in Heaven. They demonstrate God's love in words and actions when they leave a legacy gift of love, faith, hope and gratitude. Their legacy gifts glorify God because they are not just pretending to love others, they are sincerely loving them just as it says in Romans 12:9, "Don't just pretend to love others. Really love them. Hate what is wrong. Hold tightly to what is good" (NLT). This scripture reminds us love must be sincere. The best way to be genuine and sincerely love your loved ones is to leave a legacy gift.

My passion for legacy letters ignited the day I read the obituary of a client; his name was Clyde Hughes. I was impacted by the statement he left a beautiful love note for his wife in case he preceded her in death.

An obituary is a news article which reports the recent death of a person, typically along with an account of the person's life and information about the upcoming funeral. Most obituaries provide only the details about the person who died, including their birth date, date of death, and the names of their survivors. So, it was surprising to me to see the acknowledgment of what Clyde left behind—a love letter. Not only did the obituary mention the letter, but it also summarized the letter: ***"He told her how proud he was to have had her as a wife and that he had always loved her and that he would love her forever."*** The minute I read those heartfelt words from Clyde to his wife Eileen, I could no longer consider this simple suggestion as an optional task for legacy planning. I knew immediately in my heart these final words made a difference. These sincere and thoughtful words touched a grieving heart and left a legacy gift of love, faith, hope and gratitude. With permission from his daughter, you may read the obituary of Clyde Hughes and his legacy love letter in the **Appendix Sample Letters** section at the back of this book.

I interviewed Clyde's daughter while compiling the research for this book. I learned from Clyde's daughter her mother cherished the legacy letter and read it every day. Not only did she read it to herself, but she also shared it with others until the day she joined Clyde in Heaven. I was further amazed when Clyde's daughter told me her dad wrote the legacy love letter to his wife because of me. She knew this because the letter was found in the envelope with his estate plan. I had prepared the legal documents for him, and he had attended one of my legal seminars. When I was able to witness what an impact Clyde's letter had on his wife and the fact I was the one who encouraged him to complete the letter, I had the evidence I needed to prove to myself and others how important legacy love letters were. I quickly understood the significance of the opportunity to share this valuable information with my clients when advising them about their legacies.

Clyde had attended one of my legal seminars which I had hosted at my law center for clients who wanted to take extra or optional legacy planning steps even though their estate planning documents were already completed. Through my newspaper articles and local speaking engagements, I presented the extra legacy planning steps which included writing letters to loved ones; creating a list of specific gifts to named beneficiaries; and preplanning funeral and burial arrangements. I had no idea back then this simple suggestion, "You can write a letter to your loved ones," which was number seven on the top ten list of what survivors needed to know, would lead him to write a letter that inspired me to write this book and a mission to inspire others to write them. To read "Top Ten Things Your Survivors Need to Know: 20th Anniversary Edition," go to www.teplc.com/articles/topten2023.

In September 2020, I had the chance to speak for the first time about legacy love letters at a Ladies Fall Retreat at Zephyr Point Conference Center in Lake Tahoe, Nevada. Even though I had attended the Ladies Fall Retreat at the conference center in the past, I had never felt compelled to volunteer to be a speaker. But when I received the text the speaker couldn't attend due to the pandemic that year, I felt a prompt to volunteer to speak. All it took was a bit of courage and a simple text: "I can talk about love letters if you want." I had spoken to groups about estate planning, but this was my first opportunity to combine my Christian faith with my legal experience. I was assuming my audience would be ready to hear about legacy because Christians believe estate planning is wise stewardship. There was just one problem—the retreat audience was mostly Nevada residents, so I couldn't talk to them about California probate law since I was not licensed in their state. What looked like a restriction at first was instead permission to abandon what I knew about case law and codes and to focus for the first time solely on God's heart for legacy. This experience reminded me how God gives us our talents, abilities, experiences, spiritual gifts, and personality traits so we can use them to help other people for His glory.

Since this speaking opportunity was at a Christian women's retreat, I brought my Bible to the love letter presentation. I read 1 Corinthians 13:4-8 out loud and told my audience about writing love letters and God's love. I shared sample letters with them, including the first "formal" letter I ever wrote and a sweet love letter from my son when he was learning to write, which simply said "I love you" in crayon.

Sharing these letters helped me connect with my audience and emphasized the importance of letters. Unfortunately, the first "formal" letter I wrote was from a case I lost in my own household. I was seeking an increase in "alounece" (allowance) for my sisters and I, so I wrote a letter. My parents did reward the demand letter with an increase in allowance, just not the amount I had requested. However, the "formal" letter serves as a reminder of God's love for me and the talents He has given me to be used for His glory. This sample letter was clearly not a legacy love letter; it was my first legal demand letter for my first legal battle, even though I hadn't obtained my law degree yet. I felt prompted to share this letter with the audience—reading this handwritten letter with misspellings written when I was in elementary school was proof God created me to write letters. Not only that, He created me to advocate for others in both my legal career and now my passion project to help people change their hearts for legacy. To read the crayon love letter and the "alounece" letter, see **Appendix Sample Letters**.

What if everyone grieving a loved one received a legacy love letter? This exciting, God-given dream can only be fulfilled miraculously by God because it is so big I can't do it on my own. But I won't give up too soon because God gives us our gifts and calling to uniquely qualify us to do the things He created us to do. This is a big, God-sized dream for my life but not an impossible dream. I now know my legal training and experiences helping people through difficult decisions and navigating which steps to take can be used for something even more important than an earthly legacy. During the season I wrote and built this book with coaching from Dr. Brian Dixon and support from the hope*books author community, God was faithful to me and showed me how He uniquely qualified me to share this message about His heart for legacy. Until I take my last breath, I am committed to advocating this important message so our loved ones grieve with the eternal hope of Heaven and the peace and joy only God can provide. Our loved ones will still experience grief, but our legacy love letters will help them grieve differently.

Will God change your heart for legacy? This hope*book is for you if you are in the season of legacy planning, and you are seeking peace of mind and heart for both you and your loved ones. You will discover God's heart for legacy is for His wondrous works to be remembered. Expressing love, faith, hope, gratitude, encouragement, forgiveness, and sympathy demonstrates God's love in words and actions and leaves an extraordinary legacy that glorifies God. Sharing love and faith and reminding loved ones that God promises we will be reunited in Heaven encourages loved ones to seek refuge and strength in God and not the world during their journey through grief. When we recognize the brevity of life and take action to write legacy letters our loved ones will someday read, we will be remembered by leaving a legacy gift with an everlasting impact. By understanding and acting on a sense of urgency, we don't miss our opportunity to tell our loved ones how much they mean to us and how much we love them. Legacy planning provides for the health and well-being of your loved ones and helps guard their minds and hearts as they face impossible situations and problems which will grow their character.

Thank you for letting me walk beside you as you embrace the legacy God designed and created just for you. I pray God continues to bless you as He changes your heart for legacy so you can increase your efforts to love the people in your life well. You will find true fulfillment from being the person God meant you to be and sharing the life message you're meant to share with your loved ones.

With love, your friend and legacy coach,

Gwen

P.S. Since you are just getting started with writing your legacy love letters, I want to share with you a free resource I created. Go to my website: writelegacyloveletters.com or gwenchristeson.com to access a free guide on choosing the ingredients for your legacy love letter.

Chapter One

God's Heart for Legacy: Your Story is a Work of ART

God's heart for legacy is revealed in how He created each one of us to use the gifts and calling He gave us to love and serve the people in our lives. Your legacy is your story, the life you live, and the impact you make by living in pursuit of a deeper faith and a more meaningful life. His purpose for your legacy story is for His wondrous works to be remembered. Psalm 111:4 tells us, "He has caused his wondrous works to be remembered; the Lord is gracious and merciful" (ESV). He has caused His wondrous works to be remembered, including you; your story is a work of ART. Each letter in the acrostic ART represents God's plans for your life and His purpose for your legacy. God created a masterpiece, a work of ART, when he created you to be Awake, to be Real, and to Speak Truth.

Your Legacy Story

God created each one of His children for a purpose, and He has a plan for each one of us. This plan becomes your life story. This life story becomes your legacy story. Your legacy story, just like a book, will have a beginning and an end. Your legacy story may have some typos, and it may even have some chapters you do not want to read out loud, but your legacy story still belongs to you and shows how God works all things out for good. To say "God works all things out for good" isn't wishful thinking; it is a biblical promise. In fact, the Message translation of Isaiah 54 calls this statement God's decree, which means God's plan for how things will happen. Verse 17 contains God's promise, "I'll see to it that everything works out for the best." God has written your final chapter, so only God knows how and when your story will end. But we can have faith and confidence in His decree because He'll see to it that everything works out for the best. It is not too late to glorify God by living fully. You will honor Him with your legacy story when you are remembered for your faith, how you loved God, and how you loved others. Your legacy story is uniquely beautiful and proof to those you leave behind that everything works out for the best.

Your Starring Role

God is the author of your legacy story; He has created you specifically for the starring role. You were specifically created for the starring role you played in each familial relationship: a parent, a child, a sibling, a spouse. Each of these relationships influenced your identity and your story. God not only created you for this starring role, but He wants you to embrace it as you strengthen your relationships. Your relationships with God and your loved ones are vital to living fully in pursuit of a deeper faith and a more meaningful life as you use your gifts and calling to bring God glory. To play your starring role as God scripted it, you must use your gifts to serve and to love Him and to love others in words and action. I have limited acting and vocal skills, so I've never been a leading actor on stage, but I did get to play a part in *Alice in Wonderland* when my twin sister and I were cast as Tweedle Dee and Tweedle Dum. Just as the leading actor works closely with the director to ensure the performance aligns with the overall vision of the production, we are to seek God's guidance as we play our starring role as God designed and scripted it.

Good And Perfect And Irrevocable Gifts

God is the author of your legacy story; His gifts are good and perfect and irrevocable. We can trust God's plans for our life and purpose for our legacy because His gifts are good and perfect. James 1:17 promises, "Every good gift and every perfect gift is from above, coming down from the Father of lights, with whom there is no variation or shadow due to change" (ESV). This scripture reminds us not to fear change because His gifts are good and perfect. We can trust God's plans for our life and purpose for our legacy because the gifts God has given us to love and to serve Him are irrevocable. We rely on the biblical truth God is not taking our gifts and calling away from us. Romans 11:29 promises, "For the gifts and the calling of God are irrevocable" (ESV). Irrevocable means permanent, not flexible. When something is irrevocable, it cannot be changed or altered. You can live out your legacy life with confidence your gifts and calling will not be revoked, changed, or altered by God. He designed your gifts and calling especially for you to make you and your legacy story unique. He has promised He will not take your gifts and calling away from you. Even though God has promised this, it is your responsibility to use your gifts and calling to be a blessing to others and bring Him glory. All your opportunities, abilities, and resources come from God and are His handiwork. Ephesians 2:10 says, "For we are God's handiwork, created in Christ Jesus to do good works, which God prepared in advance for us to do" (NIV). Consider God's handiwork and the things which make you, you. God prepared you in advance to serve Him with your talents or spiritual gifts, your heart, your strengths and abilities, your personality, and your experiences.

Your Identification And Your Legacy Story

Your identification is part of your legacy story. As both an estate planning attorney and a notary public, I am required to obtain important information about a client and to verify their identity with proof of identification. To complete legal documents and to provide the necessary notary acknowledgment seal, I must verify they are who they say they are. I do not have to go too far back into their past because a valid driver's license or senior identification card is usually enough. Sometimes when I ask people to verify their legal name, I find out very quickly their driver's license or senior identification card doesn't always match the name they gave me on the initial paperwork for their estate plan or even the name I found on the deed to their home. It could be something simple; they have a nickname they prefer to use instead of their full legal name. At times it is their preference to be known by their middle name instead of their first name. On occasion it is adding a doctorate degree or a license. Sometimes they have added or dropped a word or numeral showing their line in succession. Each of these real-life examples demonstrate how your identification is part of your legacy story.

Your Names And Your Legacy Story

Your names are part of your legacy story, too. This part of the estate planning process is when I have some of the most captivating conversations with my clients. It's in these moments parts of their legacy story unfold as they provide the history of their names and aliases. It could be a funny story about how they acquired their nickname. It could be a charming story about their upcoming nuptials. It could be a sad story about a pending divorce or the loss of a spouse. As they share this personal information, each name adds to the story they have lived so far—their legacy. Recently I scheduled a TSA PreCheck meeting so I could verify my names and identity. I must admit I almost didn't pass the test due to a typographical error on my birth certificate. Well, to be honest, it looks like a typo because my driver's license and my passport and even my marriage certificate all have the same spelling for my first name, but my birth certificate does not match. My kindergarten teacher didn't know how to spell my full legal name so when she taught me how to write my name, she spelled it "Gwendolyn" with a "yn." When I returned home to show my mom what I had learned at school, she spotted the mistake right away. At birth, my first name was spelled "Gwendolen" with an "en." Right then and there, seeing how much I wanted the new spelling of my given name, my mom let me rewrite my name and claim the new spelling as my new identity. I have used "Gwendolyn" with a "yn" ever since. Our Heavenly Father loves us so much that He, too, lets us rewrite our names just like my mom let me rewrite my name so many years ago. It can quite simply be writing your name differently and choosing to live differently. When approving the cover for this hope*book, I decided to write my first name informally as "Gwen." As a legacy coach and advocate I wanted to use the informal, short version of my legal name so I will be more approachable as I fulfill my calling as a published Christian author and speaker. I am choosing to live differently by embracing my calling as an author and my legacy story now reflects my new name and new identity. Your names are part of your legacy story.

Your Family Tree And Your Legacy Story

Your family tree is part of your legacy story. As I prepare legal documents for my clients, I like to visualize their family tree because it represents the relationship between them and the people God has created them to be in relationship with. I must obtain full legal names and addresses for each party who will be identified in the legal documents. It is also imperative I know dates of birth, marital status, and legal heirs of each named beneficiary which is all part of their legacy story. Regardless of whom they have chosen as a beneficiary of their estate, I still must identify potential legal heirs, which include biological children and grandchildren. If my clients don't have any biological children or grandchildren, then the State of California will search for the people on their family tree to identify potential legal heirs. I evaluate the branches of the family tree and ask them if their parents are still living. I ask them if they have any siblings, living or deceased. Your family tree is a reminder of how your relationships impact your legacy story.

Your Unique Legacy Story

Your looks, likes, interests and capabilities are different and unique and add to your unique legacy story. Your legacy is the story of you, and God created you to be you; there is nobody exactly like you. The Bible even tells us God pays attention to you, down to the last detail. Luke 12:7 says, "Indeed, the very hairs of your head are all numbered" (NIV). If the very hairs on your head are numbered, it means God created you down to the last detail. If God created you down to the last detail, there is nobody like you, even if you closely resemble somebody else. I have an identical twin sister, so I can testify with personal knowledge that even though my identical twin looks just like me, we are uniquely made by God and we each have a unique legacy story. Growing up, everybody at school and in our community knew we were twins, so my twin sister and I never had a chance to trick people. As we grew older, we had a few chances to trick people who did not know us as twins. In high school, we worked at a local gym after school. We would trade-off: one of us would watch the babies in the childcare room while the other twin would take the fitness class. We found out quickly when someone was new to the gym—they would realize there were two of us because *how could this person be here taking the class when they should be taking care of the babies?* I can recall more than one occasion when somebody would look at me and then would walk—almost run—back to where their child was to make sure they had not been left unattended. There were never any injuries, but it was a small gym so we would usually laugh about it later.

Surprise encounters also happened when we worked at a clothing store connected by an opening in a shared wall. On more than one occasion the shopper would ask me a question and I knew they thought I was my twin. They would be very frustrated if I did not remember the item they had just purchased next door. With perfect timing, my twin sister would walk by at that moment, and they would realize there were, in fact, two of us who looked identical.

During college, we tricked people by accident on campus because we attended different universities and people did not know us as twins. When I was at a race to cheer for my twin sister in Santa Cruz, the team captain wanted to know why I wasn't ready to race when he saw me standing there in street clothes. The group from the UC Santa Barbara cycling team standing with me couldn't help but laugh out loud after his reprimand. One kind cyclist introduced me to the exasperated team captain just as my sister approached our group in uniform ready to race. Another incident transpired at my college graduation ceremony. My identical twin was allowed on the field with me and fellow UC San Diego graduates since she was wearing a graduation gown. Her graduation was the following day in Santa Barbara, but nobody checked her student identification card since she was wearing a cap and gown and we looked identical, so they assumed she belonged. Even at my wedding, I heard someone from my husband's engineering office asked why the bride was not wearing a wedding gown when she saw my twin sister during the ceremony. The wedding guest must have realized her mistake the moment she saw me walk down the aisle with my dad in my white gown and stand beside my maid of honor who looked just like me but was wearing pink.

The memories of these accidental twin pranks do make me smile, but I must share it was not always easy to look alike. Twins are subjected to a cruel amount of comparison. Even though we may look a lot alike on the outside, God wired us differently with our own gifts and calling. We do have similarities; we both enjoy traveling and shopping and we both are coffee fanatics. We were both wired as entrepreneurs, too. Even though my field is legal and her field is health, both of us were self-employed entrepreneurs when our children were young.

An important lesson I have learned about being an identical twin is the test of life is not who we are by comparison. The test of life is what we did with what we were given. We will be successful in our individual legacy stories when we live a life fully for God. When we choose to live an extraordinary life, not only is our life improved as we live in pursuit of a deeper faith and a more meaningful life, but our decision can influence countless generations for the glory of God.

God's Plans For Your Legacy Story

God created a masterpiece, a work of art, when He created each one of us with plans for our legacy story. Psalm 138:8 says, "The Lord will work out his plans for my life—for your faithful love, O Lord, endures forever. Don't abandon me, for you made me" (NLT). This verse reminds us we are not alone in this world because God made us and will not abandon us. His love is faithful and will endure forever. Because of His faithful and enduring love, He will work out His plans for our lives and bring us through the difficulties we face so we can use the gifts and calling He gave us to love and serve others and bring Him glory. He made you for

His glory. Isaiah 43:7 says, "everyone who is called by my name, whom I created for my glory, whom I formed and made" (NIV).

God has plans for your legacy story. Jeremiah 29:11 says, "'For I know the plans I have for you,' declares the Lord, 'plans to prosper you and not to harm you, plans to give you hope and a future'" (NIV). This verse reminds us God's plans for us are plans to prosper us and to provide hope for our future and our legacy. When we trust God with His plans for us, we are set free with the truth knowing some of our best days are still ahead because we are not home yet. God will continue writing the pages of our legacy story as we keep our focus on His plans for us. By including God's plan in our plans we can make the most of the life He specifically designed for each one of us.

Commit Your Plans To The Lord

It's easy to make plans and dreams for our lives and get too busy to be used by God. There are so many things in this world that distract us from our legacy story. They may be good things but not the best things to fulfill our life mission. The Bible tells us when we commit our plans to the Lord, our plans will succeed. Proverbs 16:3 says, "Ask the Lord to bless your plans, and you will be successful in carrying them out" (GNT). It is so easy to get distracted and to make plans to live life to the fullest without God's guidance. To succeed in glorifying God by living fully instead of just living life to the fullest, follow God's will and His plans for your life and purpose for your legacy. So remember to commit your plans to the Lord by asking Him to bless your plans.

When you commit your plans to the Lord, you can live in faith and confidence God is working together all things for good. He knows what's best and He alone can fulfill His purpose for us. Looking back at my life, I see now in the times I did not commit my plans to the Lord, I was not successful in carrying them out on my own without God's blessing. Our own plans can distract us from God's plan for our future, which is always a bigger and better plan. I learned this truth the hard way when I was laid off from my dream job. As a young associate attorney, my plan was to live and work in San Diego, California for the length of my law career. God had opened doors for me, and I had landed a sought-after position as a summer associate at a large law firm. Following the summer assignment, the same firm offered me a permanent job after graduation with a six-figure salary and big benefits. I was on the right track in fulfilling my dream—I accepted the position. I graduated from law school, and I took the bar exam. But within weeks of starting my dream job, I was laid off. Looking back now, I know it was God's plan for me to start my legal career in San Diego, but it was not His plan for me to end my legal career there. I was not committing my plans to God and asking Him to bless my plans working and living in San Diego for the entirety of my law career. So instead, I had to endure this painful experience. This painful experience was not wasted. In reflection now, I see this was God's plan for my life as I worked and gained the experience I needed so I could later establish my own law center in a different city.

God Completes The Work

Not only did God create a masterpiece, a work of art, when He created each one of us with specific plans for each of our lives and a specific purpose for each of our legacy stories, He promised to complete the work. The Bible assures us God will not abandon us. Let's read this verse in another translation because of the words chosen. Psalm 138:8 says, "You will do everything you have promised; Lord, your love is eternal. Complete the work that ***you have begun***" (GNT, emphasis mine). This translation adds value to our understanding of God's work of art—that God completes the work not only because He made us but because He has promised to complete the work He has begun. You are alive today, which proves your legacy story is not completed yet. Let God complete the work He has begun by helping you live in pursuit of a deeper faith and a more meaningful life as you commit your plans to Him and He reveals His heart for legacy.

Your Legacy Story Is Not Finished Yet

God, the author of your legacy story, knew the ending of it before it began. Just as He has written the first chapter, He has written the last chapter. But do not lose heart and quit, your legacy story is not finished yet. God wants to change your heart for legacy so you can honor Him when you are remembered for how you loved God and how you loved others. Proverbs 19:21 tells us, "Many are the plans in a person's heart, but it is the Lord's purpose that prevails" (NIV). God's purpose for your unique legacy story will prevail and you will be remembered by those you leave behind because God's plans endure forever, and His purposes last eternally. You will know when God is writing your story because it will always be filled with love, faith, hope, and gratitude.

Scripture Prompt: "Study More!"

> "He has caused his wondrous works to be remembered; the Lord is gracious and merciful." —Psalm 111:4 (ESV)

Prayer Prompt: "Pray Now!"

Dear Lord,

I am grateful for your grace and mercy and your heart for legacy. I praise you and your wondrous works and for writing my unique legacy story. Thank you for creating me as a work of art down to the last detail. Please continue to shape my mind and heart as I commit my plans to you. Help me fulfill the purpose you have for my legacy. Please complete the work you began in me and change my heart for legacy so I can honor and glorify you as I live in pursuit of a deeper faith and a more meaningful life.

Amen

Writing Prompt: "Write Now!"

Take time to reflect and write about God's heart for legacy and how He has created you as a work of art. Write about the irrevocable gifts God has given you, the unique personality traits and talents to qualify you to do the life's work He created you to do. How did your family tree and your relationships influence your identity and your story?

Worship Prompt: "Listen Now!"

"The Truth" by Megan Woods.[1]

This song reminds us we are a work of art because we can look in the mirror and know God has made us in His image. We are reminded He wouldn't change a thing about each one of us because His creation is a masterpiece, a work of art. This song also reminds us we are truly loved by God and He is proud of us, and we make Him smile. As we sing along we are boldly refuting the lies of the enemy who wants us to believe we are less than a work of art.

1 Woods, Megan. "The Truth." *The Truth*. Written by Megan Woods, Matthew West, and Jeff Fardo. Fair Trade Services, 2024, https://www.meganwoodsofficial.com/.

Chapter Two

Be Awake: Open Your Eyes To What Truly Matters—Never Be Lacking in ZEAL

When approaching legacy planning, the world asks, "What if I died today?" For a lasting legacy that honors God, Christians must answer God's question. He asks: "What if you fully lived?" To bring God glory by living fully alive, you are no longer settling for an ordinary life and legacy.

> *"The glory of God is man fully alive."*
>
> —St. Irenaeus of Lyons[2]

2 185AD, Against Heresies (Lib. 4, 20, 5-7; SC 100, 640-642, 644-648).

This popular quote reminds us when we do what God has designed us to do, that in and of itself brings God glory!

To glorify God you must be fully alive, so you need to be Awake. To be Awake, you need to open your eyes to what truly matters. To open your eyes to what truly matters, you need to be zealous, which means to never be lacking in ZEAL. Romans 12:11 directs us how to be zealous, "Never be lacking in zeal, but keep your spiritual fervor, serving the Lord" (NIV). Each letter in the acrostic ZEAL represents how to open your eyes to what truly matters and live fully for God: have Zest for life, be a faithful steward of Earthly treasures, be an Advocate for spiritual legacy, and Leave a legacy that glorifies God. This chapter focuses on how to open your eyes to what truly matters and live fully with Zest for life.

Live Fully With Zest For Life

What would your final days on Earth look like and feel like if instead of preparing to die, you made an effort to fully live? If you were making an effort to fully live, it would look like you had Zest for life. What does it mean to have Zest for life? Someone living with zest for life has enthusiasm. Zeal is enthusiasm. When you open your eyes to what truly matters, you are living with zest as you seek and know God with the expectation He will live up to His promises. As God fulfills His promises, He will reveal His plans and purpose for your life to fully live for Him and leave an impactful legacy. When your eyes are open to what truly matters, you will be Awake and able to resist the undue influence of this noisy and chaotic world. You will discover your impactful legacy when your eyes are open to what truly matters: to love God, know God, trust God, obey God, and serve God.

Work Heartily To Serve The Lord

We are called to keep our spiritual fervor serving the Lord. Fervor means dedication, commitment, and passion. To serve the Lord zealously we must have dedication, commitment, and passion, which requires us to be eager and enthusiastic. Enthusiasm requires us to work heartily. The Bible tells us when we work enthusiastically for the Lord, nothing we do is ever useless. 1 Corinthians 15:58 reminds us, "So, my dear brothers and sisters, be strong and immovable. Always work enthusiastically for the Lord, for you know that nothing you do for the Lord is ever useless" (NLT). This level of enthusiasm requires us to stand firm in our faith. God promises our work is not in vain when we devote ourselves completely to His work. But to be completely devoted requires us to work heartily and to be zealous advocates. When we excel in the work of the Lord, we strive to do our best and do more than is needed as we work wholeheartedly. When our work is not in vain it is not wasted because it is never without purpose. Everything we do for Him is worthwhile when we work for the Lord, not for people. To be zealous, give yourselves fully to the work of the Lord and work heartily because nothing you do for Him is a waste of time or effort. Colossians 3:23 directs us, "Whatever you do, work at it with all your heart, as working for the Lord, not for human masters" (NIV). This verse reminds us to work heartily and to work at it with all our heart. Leaving a legacy requires zealous advocacy, which illustrates the dedication, commitment, and passion needed to serve the Lord wholeheartedly and with zeal.

Zealous Advocate

Zealous advocacy is required in the legal profession. As a licensed attorney I must fulfill the professional conduct rules of my license which require me to do everything reasonable, within my means, to help a client achieve the goals set forth at the outset of the representation. When facing legal problems, clients contract with attorneys, who have a good working knowledge of the relevant legal issues at hand. If I am fulfilling the role as a zealous advocate, I am called to do everything necessary to win the case so long as it does not violate other ethical principles for the profession. When we have Zest for life, we are embracing the Christian life with the same amount of passion, doing everything necessary to achieve the goal of bringing God glory.

Zeal With Knowledge

We are called to work enthusiastically with dedication, commitment, and passion but we also need to have a good working knowledge. Proverbs 19:2 warns, "Even zeal is not good without knowledge, and the one who acts hastily sins" (CSB). This verse reminds us to continue to seek God as we live in pursuit of a deeper faith. To know God: spend time with Him and get to know Him by reading your Bible, worshiping Him and pouring your heart out in prayer. Proverbs 2:6 reminds us, "For the Lord gives wisdom, and from his mouth come knowledge and understanding" (NIV). By diligently studying the Word of God, your mind and heart will be opened to a deeper understanding and clearer knowledge of the truth because Jesus is the way, the truth, and the life. Knowing and embracing the truth will set you free. John 8:32 promises, "Then you will know the truth, and the truth will set you free" (NIV). Knowledge and understanding are a gift from God and our reward for living in pursuit of a deeper faith so we no longer settle for an ordinary life and legacy. Open your eyes to what truly matters and bring God glory by living fully alive with zest for life.

Scripture Prompt: "Study More!"

> "Never be lacking in zeal, but keep your spiritual fervor, serving the Lord." —Romans 12:11 (NIV)

Prayer Prompt: "Pray Now!"

Dear Lord,

Please open my eyes to what truly matters so I can discover the life and legacy I was made for and the person I was made to be. Help me never be lacking in zeal as I live in pursuit of a deeper faith and a more meaningful life. Show me each day how to live fully with zest for life so I can live fully alive to bring you glory.

Amen

Writing Prompt: "Write Now!"

Take time to reflect about having Zest for life. Write about opening your eyes to what truly matters and living fully for God with enthusiasm. Have you been asking, "What if I died today?" Now answer God's question,

"What if you fully lived?" What action will you take to commit to living fully for God so you can experience the fullness of life as our Heavenly Father designed it?

Worship Prompt: "Listen Now!"

"Plans" by Rend Collective.[3]

This song helps us proclaim out loud the biblical truth God has plans for each one of us even when we are hurting and heartbroken. Not only knowing but believing the truth God has plans for us sets our minds and hearts free as we are released from the stress of trying to figure it out on our own. When we trust God is always working we can rejoice that our story isn't over. We acknowledge God is the author of our blank pages, and we praise Him. We see God as the painter of our blank canvas, and we express gratitude. As we sing along, we are praising God for His promises, His plans and His purposes. Not only does God have plans for us, but they are greater than our wildest dreams. As we worship our Creator, we are set free to live the better story He has created for each one of us as we praise Him for His plans and confidently believe there are better days to come. As we praise Him, He will open our eyes to the things which truly matter so we can discover the life and legacy we were made for and the person we were made to be. This song reminds us to worship with a "Yes and amen" anytime we find ourselves between faith and fear. We can continue to trust in His promises, His plans and His purposes until He takes us home to Heaven.

3 Rend Collective. "Plans." *Whosoever.* Composed by Gareth Gilkeson, Matt Moher, Chris Llewellyn, Ben Glover, and Jeff Sijka. Capitol Christian Music Group, 2022, https://rendcollective.com/.

Chapter Three

Your Final Words Bring Peace of Mind and Heart

Peace of mind and peace of heart are both possible when we know and trust God with His plans for our life and His purpose for our legacy. When you plan your legacy, you bring peace of mind and heart to your loved ones because leaving a material legacy brings peace of mind and leaving a spiritual legacy brings peace of heart. This chapter focuses on how to open your eyes to what truly matters: live fully as a faithful steward of Earthly treasures and an Advocate for spiritual legacy so your final words bring peace of mind and heart.

A Good Person Leaves An Inheritance

God's heart for legacy is shown in His desire that we leave an inheritance for our children and our children's children. Proverbs 13:22 teaches "A good person leaves an inheritance for their children's children, but a sinner's wealth is stored up for the righteous" (NIV). The importance of legacy is clearly stated in this verse. When we strive to be good and glorify God, then we will leave an inheritance for our children and our children's children. To fail to leave an inheritance would be a sin since it goes against God's heart for legacy. The inheritance God has planned for us to pass on to our loved ones is a legacy of both earthly and heavenly treasures.

Putting Your Affairs In Order

We are called to put our house in order before God takes us home to Heaven. We show appreciation and gratitude to God when we fulfill our stewardship role. Putting your financial and legal affairs in order is important and brings peace of mind both for you and your loved ones. By putting your affairs in order, you will complete your legacy plan to ensure an earthly legacy of financial gifts. Writing legacy love letters is an opportunity for you to elevate your legacy planning. Instead of focusing on just an earthly legacy, you take action to focus on God's heart for legacy and the extraordinary legacy story He has already designed for you. Writing your legacy love letters brings peace of heart both for you and your loved ones.

A Faithful Steward Of Earthly Treasures

Our legacy story is fulfilled as we become good stewards of the earthly treasures God has entrusted us with. This is why faithful stewardship is a core Christian value. God is the owner of all He created and we are the stewards of His creation. We are stewards of everything God has entrusted us with, including our bodies and health, our family and friends, and our environment. Legacy letters help us fulfill our role as good and faithful stewards of the important relationships God has entrusted us with. God values our loved ones just as much as we do so we must strive to treat them with respect and care.

To glorify God by living fully requires us to fulfill our role as faithful stewards of God's resources. We naturally think that these things belong to us—our material possessions, our own lives, and our time. In pursuit of a more meaningful life and legacy, we must live in contrast with this human notion because God created the world and everything in it. Psalm 89:11 affirms the truth, "Heaven is yours, the earth also; you made the world and everything in it" (GNT).

The Bible affirms we were created to manage the earth's resources. Genesis 1:28 tells us, "God blessed them and said to them, 'Be fruitful and increase in number; fill the earth and subdue it. Rule over the fish in the sea and the birds in the sky and over every living creature that moves on the ground" (NIV).

When we fulfill our calling to be faithful stewards, God will entrust more resources to us if we show ourselves faithful with the small amounts He gives us now. In the parable of the talents or bags of gold, the owner of the "talents" called each of his servants, the stewards, to give an account of what they had done with the resources entrusted to them during the time the master had been traveling.

Matthew 25:14-30 says:

> Again, it will be like a man going on a journey, who called his servants and entrusted his wealth to them. To one he gave five bags of gold, to another two bags, and to another one bag, each according to his ability. Then he went on his journey. The man who had received five bags of gold went at once and put his money to work and gained five bags more. So also, the one with two bags of gold gained two more. But the man who had received one bag went off, dug a hole in the ground and hid his master's money. After a long time the master of those servants returned and settled accounts with them. The man who had received five bags of gold brought the other five. "Master," he said, "you entrusted me with five bags of gold. See, I have gained five more." His master replied, "Well done, good and faithful servant! You have been faithful with a few things; I will put you in charge of many things. Come and share your master's happiness!" The man with two bags of gold also came. "Master," he said, "you entrusted me with two bags of

> gold; see, I have gained two more." His master replied, "Well done, good and faithful servant! You have been faithful with a few things; I will put you in charge of many things. Come and share your master's happiness!" Then the man who had received one bag of gold came. "Master," he said, "I knew that you are a hard man, harvesting where you have not sown and gathering where you have not scattered seed. So I was afraid and went out and hid your gold in the ground. See, here is what belongs to you." His master replied, "You wicked, lazy servant! So you knew that I harvest where I have not sown and gather where I have not scattered seed? Well then, you should have put my money on deposit with the bankers, so that when I returned I would have received it back with interest. So take the bag of gold from him and give it to the one who has ten bags. For whoever has will be given more, and they will have an abundance. Whoever does not have, even what they have will be taken from them. And throw that worthless servant outside, into the darkness, where there will be weeping and gnashing of teeth." (NIV)

This parable teaches us God will entrust more resources to us if we show ourselves faithful with the small amounts He gives us now. This story helps us understand the lesson because we learn by examples. When I counsel clients or speak to large groups, I share with them case examples which bring to light how legacy planning decisions are tested in real life. Once I share with them examples of real life cases they are motivated to avoid the painful consequences. We do not automatically know how to manage God's resources. Effective stewardship is learned and requires focus and determination. In Luke 16:10, Jesus said, "Whoever can be trusted with very little can also be trusted with much, and whoever is dishonest with very little will also be dishonest with much" (NIV). We are choosing each day with our words and actions whether to be like the good servant or the lazy servant. The lazy servant was paralyzed with fear and as a result the resources that were entrusted to him were taken away. The good servant was faithful and was entrusted with more resources.

We are accountable to God for the wise and effective use of our material resources and the time we live on this earth. When we are aware of this accountability, we are motivated to rethink our use of these resources in our daily lives. Just like the servant being accountable for the bags of gold, your estate representative must report what assets they collected, what bills they paid, and how they made a distribution pursuant to your instructions. If they fail to follow the terms of the legal document, they will be in breach of their fiduciary duties. When their final report reflects a job well done, they have fulfilled their obligations well and there is closure. The best person for the job is someone who can be trusted to do the right thing. In California, the estate representative can hire help from an attorney and a tax accountant who will help guide them to do the right thing.

Managing God's Resources Wisely

We can look to the Bible and other Christians to teach us essential principles to be faithful stewards of what God entrusted to us. When the assets of your estate are passed down with minimal costs and delays, you have managed God's resources wisely during your lifetime and become a blessing to others. Resources provided by both Dave Ramsey and Crown Financial helped my husband and I learn effective stewardship with our finances throughout our marriage. For years, we have used a monthly budget and set monthly goals for tithing, saving and spending. Learning about financial stewardship led us to pay off school loans, credit cards and our mortgage so we could live a debt-free lifestyle. Because we set financial goals as a young couple, we could pay our bills and save. Because we followed through with our financial goals, we were able to communicate and agree on our top priorities, including saving for our children's college education so they could each graduate debt-free. Our children received an advance on their inheritance when they received blessings from God during our lifetime since we worked and planned responsibly. A faithful steward will be remembered for how they used money wisely by focusing on how much they can use for God's purposes, not how much they can accumulate for themselves.

Paul instructs Timothy to teach about faithful stewardship of material resources in 1 Timothy 6:17-18 , "Command those who are rich in this present world not to be arrogant nor to put their hope in wealth, which is so uncertain, but to put their hope in God, who richly provides us with everything for our enjoyment. Command them to do good, to be rich in good deeds, and to be generous and willing to share" (NIV). When we put our hope in God and help those who are in need with a willing attitude to give generously and to share everything, we will be faithful stewards of God's resources. Our lives reveal whether we are truly loving and faithful when our actions measure up to our attitudes because thoughts and words are not enough.

Here Today And Gone Tomorrow

I like to read The Message for additional understanding when I am studying God's Word. The translator's primary goal was to capture the tone of the text and the original conversational feel of the Greek, in contemporary English. 1 Timothy 6:17-19 says, "Tell those rich in this world's wealth to quit being so full of themselves and so obsessed with money, which is ***here today and gone tomorrow***. Tell them to go after God, who piles on all the riches we could ever manage—to do good, to be rich in helping others, to be extravagantly generous. If they do that, they'll build a treasury that will last, gaining life that is truly life" (MSG, emphasis mine). This interpretation of 1 Timothy 6:17-19 motivates me, especially the words "***gaining life that is truly life***." If we fulfill the purpose God has for our life, our reward is to gain life that is truly life. The directive "***Tell them to go after God***" is a call to action and a reminder for each one of us to focus on God—not on the world—as we stand committed to loving the people in our lives well and allowing Jesus to love others through us.

To bring glory to God with our life and legacy, we must truly live. To truly live, we must focus on what really matters, which is living fully and leaving a legacy that glorifies God. A faithful steward anticipates future financial needs and prepares for them. Effective stewardship requires both spending and saving money wisely so funds are available when needed. Lack of financial planning and action usually leads to problems. God provides for us, but we must also be responsible and do our part. Proverbs 20:4 warns, "A farmer too lazy to plow his fields at the right time will have nothing to harvest" (GNT). This verse reminds us to plan and act at the right time. Acting at the right time is crucial for legacy planning.

My husband and I have three adult children. When each of them turned 18 years old, I had each one of them sign a basic California estate plan which included a Last Will & Testament; an Advance Healthcare Directive, and a Power of Attorney. This is an example of how faithful stewardship results when you plan and act at the right time. My children needed these legal documents in place to avoid the cost and delay of court procedures upon their unexpected incapacity or death. Since each of my children didn't own real property or assets that exceeded $100,000, they did not need a California Trust.

If my children had not signed their Power of Attorney or their Advance Healthcare Directive, and something had happened causing their incapacity, then my husband and I would have had to petition the court to be appointed as their conservator. Since they were over the age of 18 years old, my husband and I could no longer act as their guardians. In California, a conservator is simply a court appointed power of attorney, but it results in a lengthy and costly process. By signing these important legal documents, they were fulfilling their roles as faithful stewards by planning and acting at the right time.

Faithful stewardship requires us to be committed to managing God's resources wisely during our lifetime. If done well, we can adequately provide for our needs and become a blessing to others. God's resources include the material resources God has entrusted to us during our lifetimes. As His children, we are to learn to be faithful stewards of His gifts. Then, as we live as faithful stewards, we can set an example for the next generation. My client, Clyde Hughes, who left a legacy letter to his wife Eileen, was a faithful steward of the material resources God entrusted to him during his lifetime. He and his wife hired me in 2005 to review and update their estate plan which was completed in 1992. He and his wife hired me again in 2011 to update their documents after their son predeceased them. I assist clients in updating their estate plan even if I was not the attorney who drafted the original documents. The burden is on my shoulders, if I update a document prepared by a previous attorney, I am on the hook as if I wrote the original myself. The first step in the review process is to ensure all the legal documents necessary for a comprehensive estate plan have been signed. The second step is to determine if any changes need to be made to the original documents because they have changed their mind about who they nominated to be in charge or who they named as a beneficiary. The third step is to determine if any updates need to be made due to change in circumstances which is usually a change in address or bank account. A faithful steward of God's material resources ensures their house is in order because their legal documents are in place and are reviewed and updated when necessary. They have made the inheritance of their earthly treasures easier and blessed their loved ones.

Legacy planning is stewardship because it is an intentional prioritization of the material resources God has entrusted to us during our lifetime to faithfully serve Him after our death. Jesus encouraged planning and management of God's resources. 1 Timothy 5:8 says, "Anyone who does not provide for their relatives, and especially for their own household, has denied the faith and is worse than an unbeliever" (NIV). This verse reminds us God expects us to take responsibility for our own household. As believers in Christ and faithful stewards we are called to provide for our loved ones and leave an inheritance. We can provide for our loved ones both in leaving a material legacy of financial provision and a spiritual legacy of love and faith. Legacy planning results in giving a gift which is as great a blessing to the giver as it is to the receiver.

Peaceful Assurance

Planning your legacy brings peace to you and your loved ones. As you write your final words, ask God for peace to guard your loved ones by praying: "Let your peace which surpasses all understanding guard their hearts and minds." This is a prayer which borrows words from the Bible. Philippians 4:6-7 commands us "Do not be anxious about anything, but in every situation, by prayer and petition, with thanksgiving, present your requests to God. And the peace of God, which transcends all understanding, will guard your hearts and your minds in Christ Jesus" (NIV). This verse guides us to pray and to make our requests to God with thankful hearts. Prayer gives us the freedom to ask God for help with the things we need and to thank Him for his help. We no longer have to worry about anything when we pray about everything, including leaving a legacy for our loved ones. The peace of God is what we all need to guard our hearts and minds.

The Message translation of this verse encourages us to pray instead of worrying. I appreciate this translation because it helped me understand when we replace worry with prayer, our hearts and minds will know peace. Philippians 4:6-7 says, "Don't fret or worry. Instead of worrying, pray. Let petitions and praises shape your worries into prayers, letting God know your concerns. Before you know it, a sense of God's wholeness, everything coming together for good, will come and settle you down. It's wonderful what happens when Christ displaces worry at the center of your life" (MSG). When you pray you need to let God know your concerns so He can answer with a peaceful assurance He works everything out for the good.

Supernatural Power To Transcend Time

Your legacy love letter is the last communication received by your loved one. Letters have the supernatural power to transcend time. The recipient can see your face, hear your voice and feel your love. When your last words express your love and your final goodbye, you leave a legacy with an everlasting impact. This is a legacy built with an unfailing love, an attribute of God Himself. Love is to guide all we do without exception. Your letter will love and protect your loved ones and ease the burden of pain and sorrow they are experiencing. 1 Corinthians 13:7 says that Love "always protects" (NIV).

You will ease their pain and sorrow with a heartfelt goodbye. When I think of a heartfelt goodbye, I think about a prayer and a blessing for your loved one. Numbers 6:24-26 says, "The Lord bless you and keep you; the Lord make his face shine on you and be gracious to you; the Lord turn his face toward you and give you peace" (NIV). This verse is a prayer and a blessing and a reminder of God's promise to be with us and to give us peace.

The act of letter writing is a gift to your loved ones, and your letter helps them move forward with the healing process. This is an act of kindness and love. 1 Corinthians 13:4 says, "Love is kind" (NIV). To be kind to your loved ones, you must use gentle, kind words. Proverbs

15:1 tells us, "A gentle answer turns away wrath, but a harsh word stirs up anger" (NIV). Acts of kindness and compassion have the power to inspire hope in both the giver and the recipient. My favorite definition of kindness is from Dr. Barry H. Corey, author of *Love Kindness: Discover the Power of a Forgotten Christian Virtue*. He says, "Kindness is fierce, never to be mistaken for niceness."[4] This definition resonated with me because every single yearbook message I ever received as a young girl told me how nice I was, which I didn't like, because I thought it made me weak. Corey's definition of kindness empowered me to embrace the virtue God had given me with a new understanding God had wired me specifically to be kind. Now I know I am not weak, instead I am fierce, which will never be mistaken for niceness. My kindness is God's love flowing through me so I can bless others. Corey teaches that kindness is not a soft or timid virtue, he encourages his readers that kindness is a biblical way of living. He says kindness is not a duty, instead it is the natural result of the Holy Spirit's presence in our lives.[5]

What If You Died Today?

As an advocate for legacy planning, I do not shy away from talking to people about death because it is my job to remind them it is not "*if* they die" it is "*when* they die." I am not being harsh; I am being kind by reminding them of the undeniable truth life is short, no matter how long we live. I want to share with you expert advice from my estate planning law practice. I advise my clients the best approach is to plan their estates as of right now. As I discuss and prepare an estate plan I ask each client, "What if you died today?" This helps them focus on their current circumstances and objectives so I can help them make decisions and put them in writing. We know circumstances and objectives will change in the future so I remind them they can review and update their plan at a later date if there has been a change in circumstances due to a change in marital status, a change in residence, or the birth or death of a spouse or child. The same approach helps with writing legacy love letters. Don't put off writing your letters because you might have more to

4 Corey, Barry H. *Love Kindness: Discover the Power of a Forgotten Christian Virtue*. Carol Stream, IL, Tyndale House Publishers, Inc., 2016, xx.

5 Corey, xxi.

say later. Instead, write them now and know you can write another one at a later date. Both Diane's husband and Anne's mother updated their letters. Anne's mother wrote a post script to update her letter: "***p.s. it is 7 years later 9-97 & I still stand by this message.***" Diane's husband drew a line through how many years they had been together and updated it: "***We have been together about ~~16~~ 24 years as of this date.***" To read their letters, see **Appendix Sample Letters**.

All Or Nothing Approach

When I wrote my legacy love letters to my three children, I chose to write one for each child. I chose to complete all three letters in one day because I couldn't imagine how terrible it would be if I completed only one letter and the other two children were left empty-handed. I knew immediately my approach had to be all or nothing. I couldn't leave anybody out. Writing only one letter out of three seemed worse than not writing at all. It would probably make them feel less loved or, even worse, not loved at all. Even though I wrote all three letters to my children on one day, I had spent weeks preparing for writing them. I spent time reflecting on each one of them individually and praying and asking God for guidance of how I could love them well with my final words. I chose to write one letter to each of my children but you can write just one letter. Both Ginna and Anne's mother wrote one letter to both their children. To read their letters, see **Appendix Sample Letters**.

Peace Of Heart

Legacy love letters deliver a legacy gift of love, faith, hope and gratitude and help our loved ones grieve with peace. John 14:27 tells us, "Peace I leave with you; my peace I give you. I do not give to you as the world gives. Do not let your hearts be troubled and do not be afraid" (NIV). When we receive the peace He leaves with us, our hearts will not be troubled, and we do not need to be afraid. This is peace of heart. In reviewing The Message translation of the same verse, we find it is the Holy Spirit who provides us comfort so we do not need to feel abandoned. John 14:25-27 states, "I'm telling you these things while I'm still living with you. The Friend, the Holy Spirit whom the Father will send at my request, will make everything plain to you. He will remind you of all the things I have told you. I'm leaving you well and whole. That's my parting gift to you. Peace. I don't leave you the way you're used to being left—feeling abandoned, bereft. So don't be upset. Don't be distraught" (MSG).

The Message translation reminds us God is giving us this gift of peace which leaves us well and whole. Because we receive the Holy Spirit and the gift of peace, we can be calm—we don't need to be upset or distraught. When we are distraught, we are distressed, hysterical, upset, troubled, worried, flustered, agitated, disturbed, and panic-stricken. When we are calm, we have peace. When we hold the peace of God in our hearts, it changes our mindset and our behaviors because we are well and whole. The peace of God fills our hearts and makes us calm. Pray for your loved ones to receive the Holy Spirit and the gift of peace so they can experience calm and not live their lives distressed, hysterical, upset, troubled, worried, flustered, agitated, disturbed, and panic-stricken. They will live their lives with peace of heart.

Gift Of The Holy Spirit

We are not alone here on earth because Jesus promises us the Holy Spirit to care for us and guide us. John 14:16 says, "And I will ask the Father, and he will give you another advocate to help you and be with you forever—" (NIV). This advocate is the Spirit of God Himself. The Holy Spirit is the very presence of God within us, helping us live as God wants. By our faith, we can rely on the Holy Spirit's power each day to care for us and guide us. We can look at life differently when we understand the Spirit's power—because of the Holy Spirit, we are never completely alone and never without guidance.

Winning With Good Counsel

The Bible reminds us good counsel is needed to win. Proverbs 24:5-6 says, "It's better to be wise than strong; intelligence outranks muscle any day. Strategic planning is the key to warfare; to win, you need a lot of good counsel" (MSG). Legacy planning is considered strategic planning because you are putting your affairs in order before it is too late. You are making it easier for your loved ones to succeed despite the unfortunate circumstances. Estate planning helps provide for your loved ones to make sure they are not overwhelmed with legal and financial obligations and obstacles upon your passing. There are a lot of steps to take to put your affairs in order, so counsel of an attorney is recommended to provide the direction, counsel, and wisdom needed. As an estate attorney I work directly with my clients and seek help from both their financial and tax advisors. I perform my role but I cannot do it alone because we each have a part to play in the overall process.

Leaving A Positive Legacy

Author Gary Chapman is well known for identifying the five love languages to help us express affection to loved ones in the way they interpret as love. He also co-authored a book with Ross Campbell, MD called *How To Really Love Your Adult Child.*[6] This is a must-read for parents of adult children because the authors drew from their counseling practices, family research, and their own experiences as parents to make a practical handbook for parents concerned with developing positive, growing relationships with their young adult children.[7] As a legacy advocate, Chapter 10 resonated with me. It is called "Leaving Your Child A Positive Legacy." The authors identify the three nonmaterial legacies that greatly influence our children and their character: a moral legacy; a spiritual legacy; and an emotional legacy. They write, "All the legacies we leave our children will affect their personal character."[8]

In considering how you can leave a positive legacy for your loved ones, I agree with the authors that those who have been given a positive moral legacy receive a valuable asset for future living. Campbell and Chapman explain:

> As with all legacies, a moral legacy becomes the property of your children when you die. It is theirs to enjoy or endure. From the legacy, they receive encouragement

6 Campbell, Ross, and Gary Chapman. *How To Really Love Your Adult Child.* Chicago, IL, Northfield Publishing, 2011.

7 Campbell and Chapman, 12.

8 Campbell and Chapman, 170.

> or disappointment. Negative or positive, your children have no choice but to receive your legacy. What they do with it, of course, is their responsibility. Those children who have been given a positive moral legacy receive a valuable asset for future living. Conversely, those who are given a negative moral legacy receive a liability with which they must learn to cope.[9]

Your legacy letter is an opportunity to share your faith with your loved ones—this is your spiritual legacy. The authors recommend it might help to think about how you want to communicate your religious beliefs so your loved ones will receive a spiritual legacy. They write, "The person who says, 'I believe there is a heaven and that eventually everyone will go there' is expressing his own beliefs in what exists beyond the material world."[10] Later, Campbell and Chapman continue, "The spiritual needs of our children are great; and passing on a spiritual legacy gives them significance, purpose, and noble values that can benefit future generations."[11] Our legacy love letters leave a spiritual legacy which gives our loved ones' significance, purpose, and noble values that can benefit future generations.

Scripture Prompt: "Study More!"

> "Anyone who does not provide for their relatives, and especially for their own household, has denied the faith and is worse than an unbeliever." —1 Timothy 5:8 (NIV)

9 Campbell and Chapman, 172.

10 Campbell and Chapman, 173.

11 Campbell and Chapman, 175.

Prayer Prompt: "Pray Now!"

Dear Lord,

You teach us that anyone who does not provide for their relatives has denied the faith and is worse than an unbeliever. Please help us take action and the necessary steps for legacy planning so our attitude and behaviors are pleasing to you and are in alignment with your heart for legacy and your plan for stewardship of both our earthly and heavenly treasures.

Amen

Writing Prompt: "Write Now!"

Journal and reflect about your stewardship goals for all your resources, both earthly and heavenly treasures. During this time of reflection, do not get discouraged; there is still time to change your plans and your strategy for managing God's resources. As you journal, consider the difference between your earthly and heavenly treasures. Your earthly treasures leave a material legacy, which requires both legal and financial arrangements and your heavenly treasures leave a nonmaterial legacy which is moral, spiritual and emotional.

Worship Prompt: "Listen Now!"

"The Blessing" by Elevation Worship[12]

The lyrics, "The Lord bless you and keep you"[13] is an example of a heartfelt goodbye. The words of this song are a prayer for our loved ones. As we sing along, we are asking for a blessing for our loved ones so His favor is upon them for a thousand generations. We are reminded whether we are rejoicing or weeping, God is for us. God's presence goes before us and behind us, and beside us and gives us peace.

12 Elevation Worship. "The Blessing (Morning & Evening)." *Graves into Gardens: Morning & Evening*. Written by Kari Jobe, Cody Carnes, Steven Furtick, Chris Brown. Capitol Christian Music Group, 2020, https://www.elevationworship.com/.

13 Elevation Worship. "The Blessing (Morning & Evening)."

Chapter Four

Help Your Loved Ones Grieve With Peace and Joy

God designed us to be people loving and living for Him. This chapter focuses on how to Leave a legacy that glorifies God by helping your loved ones grieve with peace and joy because our love letters help them find faith and hope in God again.

Our Letters Impact Heavy Hearts

Grief is the most painful emotion we go through in life. During times of grief, our hearts are heavy with sorrow. Psalm 119:28 says, "My soul is weary with sorrow; strengthen me according to your word" (NIV). Earlier in this book I shared the story of my client, Clyde Hughes, who left a legacy letter to his wife Eileen. Clyde's legacy story illustrates the powerful impact of final words. His legacy love letter was a gift from the heart and comforted his wife's heavy heart. When his letter had an impact on his wife's heavy heart, she shared his final words which became a lifeline to her and those she encountered as she lived out her final days on this side of Heaven. I know for sure Clyde was standing there to meet her when she arrived.

Your final words help your loved ones remember what God says about them when they cannot hear or listen in their own strength. Clyde's legacy letter illustrates this too. When he told her how proud he was to have had her as a wife and he had always loved her and he would love her forever his final words reminded her she was loved by him and by God. Your final goodbye leaves an everlasting impact because legacy love letter recipients take hope in knowing God controls their future. During their grief journey, they can turn toward God to be their hope, comfort, and source of abundant joy.

Give Them Health And Well-being

A legacy letter helps our loved ones grieve differently, which positively impacts their health and well-being. Our religious beliefs and our faith in God impact all areas of our life. But more specifically, our personal values are at the core of our being and influence our health and well-being. Our faith-infused words bring salt and light to our loved ones during their grief journey which helps them grieve with peace and joy.

Give Them God's Perfect Peace

Our final words help our loved ones listen to God's powerful voice so they can grieve with peace and joy and the hope of Heaven. When our grieving loved ones trust God, their minds and hearts will be steadfast, and they will grieve with the perfect peace of God. Isaiah 26:3 says, "You will keep in perfect peace those who trust in you, all whose thoughts are fixed on you!" (NLT). God's perfect peace is what our hearts long for. When our loved ones place their trust in God, He will give them the perfect peace necessary to overcome any obstacles and challenges they face during their grief journey. Your final words help them keep their thoughts anchored in God's love so they can maintain their focus on

God and His promises. When they maintain their focus on God and His promises, their minds and hearts will be steadfast, and they will not turn away from Him.

Give Them Freedom

When our loved ones focus on God's Word, it leaves no room for negative thoughts or emotions. Only God can set our loved ones free from all confusion and bring clarity of mind. We want our loved ones to be obedient, bright, healthy, happy, and productive. We want our loved ones to live a godly life which pleases God. When our loved ones live fully for God, they too can leave an extraordinary legacy.

Help God Rescue Their Crushed Spirits

God grieves with us and rescues those whose spirits are crushed. Psalm 34:18 promises, "The Lord is close to the brokenhearted; he rescues those whose spirits are crushed" (NLT). God blesses our broken hearts and brings us to a place of healing. When someone is poor in spirit, they are experiencing sadness or disappointment. They lack spirit because their grief has drained them spiritually. We do not lose heart when we are drained mentally, physically, and spiritually, because our Heavenly Father rescues us. We can humbly depend on Him instead of ourselves. We know what it feels like to grieve and to be crushed in spirit so we want our legacy love letters to help God rescue our loved ones.

Help Them Embrace A New Identity

We must show grace to our loved ones during their season of loss and grief. We don't want to minimize their pain or rush them through their grief journey. They are not only crushed in spirit, but they are also struggling with a new identity. The late H. Norman Wright was a grief and trauma therapist in private practice for over thirty years. His impressive resume includes director and professor roles at both Biola University and Talbot School of Theology. He authored over one hundred books including *Experiencing Grief*. His purpose for writing this book was to help readers progress through the grief journey with a greater sense of comfort and hope.[14] His expertise and his counseling experience helping grieving people in their grief journey resulted in a practical and healing guide for those journeying through the experience of the loss of a loved one.

In experiencing the loss of a loved one, Wright helps his readers understand how a season of grief can result in a struggle with a new identity. Wright explains:

> Prior to the death of your loved one, your life was going in a well-established direction. This has changed. You had an identity. You could say who you were. This too has changed. You are not exactly who you were. The person you lost was part of your identity. You were someone's mother or aunt or spouse or brother. You continue to be that person in your heart and memory, but there's a vacant place where your loved one stood. And the loss of this person has subtracted from you part of who you were.[15]

Wright's explanation and insight regarding the old and new identity resonated with me because our relationships are so important to who we are and how we live our lives. I see this when I am counseling my clients following the loss of a loved one. Wright further explains why the loss of a sibling deserves even more understanding. "There is no other loss in our society that is so neglected as the death of a brother or sister. When you lose a sibling, you lose a person who is a part of your formative past, someone who has been in your life a long time."[16] This loss of a person who is part of our identity is another reason why grief is so challenging. When we leave a final goodbye to our loved one who is grieving the loss of a person who is part of their identity they won't feel alone or neglected. Your legacy letter becomes a source of comfort and aid to them and their grieving hearts so you can continue to be that person in their heart and memory.

---

14 Wright, H. Norman. *Experiencing Grief.* Nashville, TN, B&H Publishing Group, 2004, iv.

15 Wright, 22.

16 Wright, 15.

Help Them Walk With Jesus

Mark Medley, a pastor and a fellow hope*books author wrote *Walking Through Grief,* a beautiful tribute to his wife Melissa, as God healed his grieving heart after thirty-five years together. Despite his grief, he still thanked God for the gift of his time with his beloved wife and friend. He was able to celebrate what they had together as he mourned her loss. In his personal story he showed his readers how God equipped him to walk with Jesus and with grief at the same time. He wrote, "In my loss, I can walk with Jesus and with grief at the same time – and the Holy Spirit will guide us on this journey down a roadway called lament."[17] Mark identifies and discusses common mile markers in grieving the loss of a spouse.[18] His best advice for grieving hearts is to turn toward God, not away from God. As you write your legacy love letter, I pray your loved ones follow Mark's advice and turn toward God not away from God. Your heartfelt goodbye is instrumental in helping your loved ones turn toward God during their season of intense emotional suffering. Mark says, "Staying close to God is essential in order to grieve and move forward in a healthy way."[19]

Help Them Sit With God

Natasha Smith's book, *Can You Just Sit With Me? Healthy Grieving for the Losses of Life,*[20] helped me personally when I was seeking to understand grief and how to honor God during my season of grief. Through her own experiences of loss and growth, she provides a faith-based road map for readers to navigate their grief journey. Natasha provides biblical and practical wisdom to sit with the brokenhearted and experience God's healing grace. She points her readers to the God of comfort and hope.

Your legacy love letters help your loved ones find faith and hope in God again during their season of grief. Natasha says grief is a process we

---

17 Medley, Mark. *Walking Through Grief.* Matthews, NC, hope*books, 2023, 9.

18 Medley, 134-137.

19 Medley, 136.

20 Smith, Natasha. *Can You Just Sit With Me? Healthy Grieving for the Losses of Life.* Santa Rosa, CA. InterVarsity Press, 2023.

must work through, and God wants us to know we are not alone. She discovered it was not a matter of getting over it, but of allowing God to help her through it. She relies on Psalm 46:10, "Be still, and know that I am God" (NIV). She says this verse is God's invitation to us asking, "Can you just sit with me?"[21] By sharing her story, Natasha encourages her readers to work through the process of grief just like she did. "God is asking us if we can just sit with him in this time, in this grief, in this hard place, and in this pain to listen and to know that he is God."[22] I believe your heartfelt goodbye reminds your loved ones of God's presence as He invites them to listen and know He is God even when He is helping them through the process of grief. Your letters help your loved ones and encourage them to grieve with peace, joy, and hope as you encourage them to allow God to help them through their season of grief. I pray for your loved ones, and I pray they hear God ask, "Can you just sit with me?"

God will continue to love your loved ones during their season of grief. Your loved ones can turn toward God, and He will rescue them. He loves them and is ready to be their comforter and friend. God provides wisdom and discernment to help them through their grief emotions of anger, pain and joy. Only God can bring your loved ones to a place of healing by restoring their souls.

Natasha reminds us what we say is important during times of grief: "Because our words are powerful and bring either life or death, what we say is important during times of grief. Being intentional with our words, being gentle with ourselves, and extending grace to ourselves and others are important."[23] In her book, Natasha provides a list of affirmations which can be used daily including "I receive God's love and hope for me today."[24] Her list of affirmations are designed to allow us to acknowledge and make space for grief while gently leaning into our healing. Her list of affirmations will inspire you to pray an affirmation over your loved one or incorporate an affirmation into your legacy love letters.

21 Smith, 38.

22 Smith, 38.

23 Smith, 152.

24 Smith, 152.

Help Them Find Rest

As you help your loved ones grieve differently, you can remind them to take time to rest and care for their souls. Natasha teaches, "Because grief is draining – mentally, physically, and spiritually – take time for rest."[25] Natasha explains resting within our souls means refilling ourselves with God's Word, worship, and His presence. She says, "As we sit, the most important thing we can do is to care for our souls."[26] Our loved ones will grieve differently if they can rest and care for their souls by refilling themselves with God's Word, worship and presence. You can encourage your loved ones to rest and care for their souls by writing, "I know that you will walk through the process of grief, and it will be draining on you mentally, physically, and spiritually, so please remember to take time to rest."

Natasha recognizes we will not ignore or forget our grief. She writes, "Now, this does not mean we forget about our grief. It also doesn't mean our grief is pushed to the side, stuffed, or ignored. No, it simply means as we sit in the presence of the Lord, we will feel the hope of Jesus arise, and we will feel his peace and comfort dwell on the inside as we grieve. It means even as we are hurting, we will sense and know everything will be all right."[27] Her words remind us eternal hope provides peace as we grieve.

Natasha gives Christians permission to grieve without questioning the strength of their faith because even though Christians grieve with the hope of Heaven, Christians still grieve. She reminds us, "Whether you are a Christian or not, grief is grief. You have the right to grieve, and grief is not an indicator of weak faith."[28]

As we try to understand what our loved ones will be facing, it is helpful to understand the current culture. Natasha explains, "Common now in our culture is the notion that grief lasts forever, and therefore grief

25 Smith, 156.

26 Smith, 157-158.

27 Smith, 158.

28 Smith, 131.

is love."[29] But Natasha reminds us the Bible views grief as temporary. She concludes this belief that grief lasts forever is not a biblical idea. She declares: "Grief is not love. God is love."[30] The goal for your legacy love letters is to help your loved ones grieve differently. Because they have received a final goodbye, they will grieve with peace, joy and hope. As you provide love and encouragement to them, you can rest in the biblical truth God is love and grief is not love. Your final words will have an everlasting impact as you encourage them to love God despite their grief.

Help Them Respond Properly

Your legacy letter helps your loved ones respond to loss properly. Natasha Smith quotes Zig Ziglar who says, "It is how we respond to loss that matters. That response will largely determine the quality, the direction, and the impact of our lives."[31] Knowing it is how we respond to loss that matters, she reminds us Jesus is with us through the process, "When the heart is hurting, Jesus is the only one who can fix it. Grieving is a journey. There's no right or wrong way to grieve. However, we don't want to be destructive or harmful to ourselves or others on this journey."[32]

When your loved one receives a legacy letter from you, it is all they need to grieve differently. They will be anchored in God's love because they have a legacy love letter they can hold onto. Your loved one's response to losing you will determine the quality, the direction, and the impact of their lives. Your legacy letter gives your loved one permission to grieve but also helps them walk with Jesus. You won't be there in person to love them, but your final words will provide support and encouragement and will be read at the times they need it most.

---

29 Smith, 140.

30 Smith, 141.

31 Ziglar, Zig. *Confessions of a Grieving Christian.* Nashville, TN, Thomas Nelson, 1999, 9, quoted in Smith, 139.

32 Smith, 139.

Help Them Breathe

My friend Anne Watson told me when she found the letter following her mother's passing, she discovered she could breathe again. Breathing is an indication of life itself. If we don't breathe, we cannot continue to live. It seems so simple but a perfect example of what happens when we are facing the loss of a loved one; like Anne, our loved ones may find it difficult to just breathe. Our final words help them breathe and continue to live so they can love God despite their grief.

Help Them Find God

The hurt and weight of grief is overwhelming, so we help our loved ones by helping them find God. God will carry them when they cannot stand on their own. Your final words enable them to see God's light at their darkest hour. By turning toward God, our loved ones will find healing and long-term relief for their pain and suffering. The world offers only temporary delights which provide short-term relief from doubt, fear, and loneliness. Temporary delights such as caffeine, alcohol, excessive shopping or binge eating do not bring everlasting joy and comfort. When your loved ones turn toward God, they will experience everlasting joy and comfort because knowing God drives away doubt, fear, and loneliness. Your loved ones will be encouraged to turn toward God and away from vices which lead to neglecting God and others. God's everlasting joy and comfort will forever impact their health, well-being, and legacy. Your legacy letters help your loved ones resist evil influences and destructive behavior during their season of grief. Continue to pray for them, God will provide the discernment they need daily to understand the clear choice between life-giving and life-destroying behaviors. Your words will encourage them to choose the right path into a secure and good future instead of the path which leads to a dead end. We want our loved ones to turn toward God in their grief so they can see clearly and distinguish between good and evil and right and wrong.

Help Them Love God

Natasha Smith points us to the God of comfort and hope so we can call and cry out to God in our grief. She explains some Christians believe because they have Jesus they shouldn't grieve, she gives permission to grieve and love God. She writes, "And though I still grieve, I know that I am perfectly loved by God. And I know though you grieve, you are perfectly loved by God. Because you can do both: you can grieve and love God."[33] Our legacy letters give them permission to do both.

We find the fullness of joy in God's presence. God promises He will show us the path of life. Psalm 16:11 says, "You will show me the path of life; In Your presence is fullness of joy; At Your right hand are pleasures forevermore" (NKJV). This verse teaches us when we are near to God and in His presence, we will be filled with joy. The theme of Psalm 16 is the joy and benefits of a life lived in companionship with God. God allows us to enjoy these benefits now and eternally. Psalm 16:8 reminds us to keep our eyes on the Lord, "I keep my eyes always on the Lord. With him at my right hand, I will not be shaken" (NIV). Believers are not exempt from the day-to-day circumstances of life but we have a unique sense of security during times of pain, trouble and failure. In comparison, unbelievers experience hopelessness about life and confusion over their true purpose on earth when they undergo times of pain, trouble and failure. Pray over your loved ones for God to show them the path of life so they can find His presence and receive the fullness of joy. As they keep their eyes on the Lord, they will not be shaken despite their times of pain.

Help Them Grieve Differently With God

Grief fills us with pain and desperation, which forces us to turn toward God or away from God. We write legacy love letters so our loved ones will grieve differently because our letters lead them to a place of healing with permission to grieve. We encourage our loved ones to turn toward God as their comforter and friend and away from worldly comforts which offer only temporary relief. As painful emotions surface, we ask God to bless our loved ones and to provide wisdom and discernment to navigate them through their grief journey. We hope and pray they overcome the loss by praying specifically God will equip them to walk with Jesus and grief at the same time. If their grieving hearts can turn toward God and not away from God, then we can be confident they will eventually move

33 Smith, 128.

forward with living fully to glorify God. They can resume living their life with faith and confidence knowing God is working together all things for good.

Our letters increase our witness and influence with our loved ones as we encourage them to fill their minds and to meditate on things that are best, not the worst; the beautiful, not the ugly; things to praise, not things to curse. A legacy love letter reminds our loved ones of the best of times, not the worst of times, by capturing personal values, family stories and life perspectives.

We want to be there for our loved ones during their time of grief. When they read your legacy love letter, they can hear your voice, see your face, and feel your love. Your legacy love letter helps them turn toward God. With a legacy love letter in their hands, our loved ones are reminded of God's presence. As they journey through grief, we want them to have a healthy mindset, which is the right attitude, a sound mind, and a heart for legacy. Pray for your loved ones as you write your legacy love letters and ask God to help them fill their minds and to meditate on things that are best, not the worst; the beautiful, not the ugly; things to praise, not things to curse. Some legacy authors even include their prayers for their loved ones in their letters. Pray God gives your loved one wisdom about what they allow into their mind. Pray for discernment, especially since the lines between good and bad are not clearly seen during times of grief and confusion. Their faith in God will bring them joy where there is sadness and depression. Only God's presence can erase all loneliness. Only God's love can dissolve all fear. Ask God to give your loved ones peace, patience, and forgiveness to replace all anger they are experiencing as they walk through their grief journey. You can pray for their healing, protection, and salvation.

Help Them Grieve Differently With Joy

Is joy possible during a season of grief? It is possible when we have a constant relationship with Jesus Christ. John 15:11 says, "I have told you this so that my joy may be in you and that your joy may be complete" (NIV). This translation promises our joy may be complete, but when we compare this verse in another translation, we can see our joy is not only complete, but it is overflowing. John 15:11 reveals the joy of the Lord not only fills us to completion but can overflow and spill over, "I have told you these things so that you will be filled with my joy. Yes, your joy will overflow!" (NLT). When we are filled with joy, we are complete, even if we are undergoing a difficult season of loss and grief. Diane's husband reminded her of joy when he wrote, ***"Please remember our laughter and the wonderful things we shared. We will share them again someday."*** Grace's husband's best friend reminded her of joyful memories collected during their 56 years of friendship. He expressed his condolences with a heavy heart and thanked God for their friendship. He wrote, "***We used to joke to others that, 'We're not friends, we're just roommates,' when in reality we were both roommates & great friends.***" To read their letters, see **Appendix Sample Letters**.

Help Them Grieve Differently With Strength

Our loved ones will grieve differently with strength when they turn toward God. Nehemiah 8:10 says, "Do not grieve, for the joy of the Lord is your strength" (NIV). During their difficult grief journey, they will find strength in their joy when they turn toward God. To succeed in getting through their grief season they will have strength because Jesus Christ will strengthen them. Philippians 4:13 says, "I can do all this through Him who gives me strength" (NIV). When they rely on Christ for their strength, they can do all things which means they can face all obstacles that come their way as they persevere and finish the race God designed specifically for them despite every hard thing they are facing. With God's power and strength, they will be loved through it all. God will not abandon them in their pain as He loves them through it all.

When the apostle Paul wrote the book of Thessalonians, he wanted the Thessalonians to understand that death is not the end of the story. Paul was writing to the Thessalonians because they were wondering why many of their fellow believers had fallen asleep, or died, and they wanted to know what would happen to them when Jesus Christ returned. The purpose of Paul's letter writing was to strengthen the Thessalonian Christians in their faith and give them the assurance of Christ's return. Some thought Christ would return immediately, so they were confused when their loved ones died because they expected Christ to return beforehand. Paul's letter writing reminds us why legacy love letters are so important. When we write letters to encourage our loved ones after we're gone, their faith can be strengthened as we provide assurance of God's love for them and His plans for their lives and purpose for their legacy.

Help God Capture Their Hearts, Minds And Souls

Our legacy letters to our loved ones ensure God has captured their hearts, minds and souls. If our loved ones have faith and their minds are captured by God, then we have confidence their faith will replace all doubt and God's love will dissolve all fear. When they continue living with a sound mind and a heart that trusts God, then we have assurance they will continue to live fully to bring God glory. The only way to bring God glory is to live a life with a sound mind and the right attitude. When they strive to be transformed by the renewing of their mind, they will not conform to this world. They can live a life which is good and acceptable to God. God's plan for their life and purpose for their legacy is the perfect will of God.

Give Them The Hope Of Heaven

Legacy letters help your loved ones grieve with peace, joy and hope by providing support and comforting words during their time of grief. Grieving with the hope of Heaven helps your loved ones know death is not the end of the story. Your legacy love letter will encourage your loved ones and give them hope, then they will not grieve like the rest of men who have no hope. 1 Thessalonians 4:13 says, "Brothers and sisters, we do not want you to be uninformed about those who sleep in death, so that you do not grieve like the rest of mankind, who have no hope" (NIV).

Biblical truth heals heavy and broken hearts with the good news death is not the end of the story. Believers in Christ are encouraged knowing the biblical truth that when Christ returns, all believers, dead and alive, will be reunited, never to suffer or die again. We can trust God and God's words found in the Bible. Our faith in God is the source of our confidence and hope which sets us apart from the rest of men who don't believe.

When writing letters, Paul wanted the Thessalonians to understand that death is not the end of the story. When Christ returns, all believers—dead and alive—will be reunited, never to suffer or die again. We should comfort and reassure each other with this great hope, just as the apostle Paul comforted the Thessalonians with the promise of the resurrection. You give hope to your loved ones with reminders you will see them again. Ginna wrote, ***"I will see you in another place many years from now."*** Diane's husband wrote, "***We are all waiting for you and watching over you.***" Anne's mother wrote, ***"We'll be together soon—it is God's promise."*** To read their letters, see **Appendix Sample Letters**.

Help Them Cry No More

Our hope comes from our Creator, the maker of heaven and earth. The Bible promises there will be no more death or mourning or crying or pain. Revelation 21:4 tells us, "He will wipe every tear from their eyes. There will be no more death or mourning or crying or pain, for the old order of things has passed away" (NIV). When we commit to writing legacy love letters, it is from our desire to help our loved ones and to do everything in our power to help them live fully for God so they can join us in Heaven someday. When we get to Heaven, we will cry no more. We will rejoice with our loved ones when we are reunited with those who have gone on before us. Knowing God will wipe every tear from our eyes brings comfort to our earthly hearts aching with the pain and suffering which follows loss. This verse reminds us to help them keep their eyes on eternity. They will be able to continue their own life journey with an eternal lens, not an earthly lens, as they hold God's promises in their heart. The promise of Heaven—no more death or mourning or crying or pain—brings comfort.

God Will Carry Them

When I was going through a long and difficult season of grief following loss of property due to a flood; the loss of my identical twin sister to estrangement; and the loss of my dad who died suddenly following a stroke, I knew God was carrying me. I reread a poem which caught my attention as a young girl even before I asked Jesus into my heart. When

I was young, my sisters and I liked to shop at our local Hallmark store while our mom was grocery shopping. It was during one of these visits to shop the Hello Kitty display or to choose our favorite Mrs. Grossman stickers when I was attracted to a nearby poster, an image of footprints in the sand. I was mesmerized by the poem which accompanied it, the "Footprints" poem. I am convinced now when I read the poem for the first time years ago, God planted a mustard seed of faith in my heart. This mustard seed of faith was small, but it carried with it the undeniable truth there was a Creator of Heaven and earth who promised to carry me when needed. The image of the footprints in the sand and the words which accompanied it spoke to my heart and offered me comfort.

Help Them Seek God's Control

During times of grief, our loved ones are experiencing loss, which makes their lives feel chaotic. Our loved ones will grieve with hope when they are reminded God is in control even in the midst of the turmoil and disorder they are experiencing. You can write, "Don't forget God is in control, even right now when things may feel chaotic."

Help Them Avoid Despair

Your legacy love letters help your loved ones avoid despair because they can grieve with eternal hope. Lee Strobel, the author of many books, including *The Case for Hope: Looking Ahead With Confidence and Courage,* reminds his readers to cling to hope to avoid despair. "We must, with God's help, learn to cling to that rare and wonderful thing called hope. Otherwise, we're destined for despair."[34] When our loved ones cling to hope, they can avoid despair which brings with it hopelessness and anguish.

Help Them Find Comfort

God promises He will be with us during our times of trouble. Isaiah 43:2 says, "When you pass through the waters, I will be with you; and when

34 Strobel, Lee. *The Case for Hope: Looking Ahead With Confidence and Courage.* Grand Rapids, MI. Zondervan 2015, 2022, 3.

you pass through the rivers, they will not sweep over you. When you walk through the fire, you will not be burned; the flames will not set you ablaze" (NIV). As you write your legacy love letters, know God is with you so be comforted by His love. Your loved one needs to be reminded they are not alone. You can pray this verse over them as you write your letter. You can write this verse in your letter by writing: "The love of God will be there to comfort you no matter what you face. He will be there to guide you through deep waters, He will tether you in the river's current, and He will protect you from the fire's flames."

You can also borrow words from the Easy English Bible translation of this verse, "When you go through deep water, I will be with you. When you cross dangerous rivers, you will not drown. When you walk through fire, it will not burn you. The flames will not destroy you" (Isaiah 43:2, EASY). As you write your final words, just change "I" to "God" and you can write: "Find comfort in ***God's promise that*** when you go through deep water, ***He*** will be with you. When you cross dangerous rivers, you will not drown. When you walk through fire, it will not burn you. The flames will not destroy you."

The Good News Translation offers more encouraging words. Isaiah 43:2 says, "When you pass through deep waters, I will be with you; your troubles will not overwhelm you. When you pass through fire, you will not be burned; the hard trials that come will not hurt you" (GNT). Again, as you write your final words, just change "I" to "God" and you can write: "When you pass through deep waters, ***God*** will be with you; your troubles will not overwhelm you. When you pass through fire, you will not be burned; the hard trials that come will not hurt you." Your final words will help your loved ones grieve with peace and joy and the hope of Heaven.

Scripture Prompt: "Study More!"

> "Brothers and sisters, we do not want you to be uninformed about those who sleep in death, so that you do not grieve like the rest of mankind, who have no hope."
> – 1 Thessalonians 4:13 (NIV)

Prayer Prompt: "Pray Now!"

Dear Lord,

I praise you today for being my source of confidence and hope. You are faithful to your children, and you draw close to the brokenhearted. You have set me apart from the rest of men who don't believe and have no hope. Thank you for helping me leave a legacy gift to help my loved ones grieve differently as they grieve with hope. Please surround them with your love and fill them with your peace and joy.

Amen

Writing Prompt: "Write Now!"

Journal and reflect about God's faithfulness and presence during your life. Reflect on times He provided confidence and hope to you, especially times when you felt He was carrying you and leaving only one set of footprints in the sand. Write out your prayers for your loved ones asking God to be with your loved ones so they find comfort in His promises.

Worship Prompt: "Listen Now!"

"Still Waters (Psalm 23)" by Leanna Crawford[35]

The lyrics Leanna Crawford sings remind us of God's promises and the fact His words have been true every season of our lives, even though we walk through the valley of the shadow of death. Because God is with us as a Father and a friend our loved ones can grieve differently. He promises goodness and mercy to follow us all of our days. This song illustrates God's desire and willingness to help our loved ones grieve with peace and joy. Still Waters reminds us our Heavenly Father will give them strength.

35 Crawford, Leanna. "Still Waters (Psalm 23)." *Still Waters*. Written by Leanna Crawford, Jonathan Gamble, and Justin Mark Richards. Provident Label Group, 2024, https://www.leannacrawford.com/.

PART TWO

WHAT LEGACY MATTERS:
LOVE GOD AND LOVE OTHERS

"So now I am giving you a new commandment: Love each other. Just as I have loved you, you should love each other."
—John 13:34, NLT

Chapter Five

Be REAL: The Right Attitude for an Impactful Legacy

To love God and to love others is the legacy that matters. The right attitude for an impactful legacy that reflects your heart is to be REAL. God created a masterpiece, a work of ART, when he created you to be REAL. You achieve an extraordinary life and legacy when your heart reflects the real you, the person God created you to be. Proverbs 27:19 reminds us, “As a face is reflected in water, so the heart reflects the real person” (NLT). When you commit your life and the time you have left investing in loving God and loving others, your heart will reflect God’s love and faithfulness and everything else will fade into the background. God’s heart for legacy is to love you, save you, and see you fulfill His plans for your life and His purpose for your legacy. To glorify God, let your legacy reflect your heart—the real you, the person God created you to be. The right attitude to be the person God created you to be is to say, "Yes, Lord I want to be real and love others the way you have loved me so my legacy reflects my heart. Show me how to glorify you with my legacy."

Love God And Love Others

The right attitude for an impactful legacy is to love God and love others. There is no need to make legacy planning complicated. You are created to leave an extraordinary legacy for your loved ones by simply loving God and loving others. When we love God and each other deeply, our lives will have more meaning. When our lives have more meaning, we leave an impactful legacy. When we leave an impactful legacy we have fulfilled God's purpose for legacy, for His wondrous works to be remembered. Our legacy will bring glory to God as we live with the right attitude: living God's way so our hearts reflect God's love.

Live And Commit To Bear Fruit

The right attitude for an impactful legacy is to live and commit to bear fruit. By bearing the fruit of the Spirit, our hearts will reflect God's love and faithfulness and we will be remembered for our love. To glorify God by living fully, be "fruity" by bearing the fruit of the Spirit. Galatians 5:22-23 tells us, "But the fruit of the Spirit is love, joy, peace, forbearance, kindness, goodness, faithfulness, gentleness and self-control. Against such things there is no law" (NIV). When living in pursuit of a deeper faith and a more meaningful life, this list of virtues helps us define the right attitudes we should possess and the right actions we should be taking. As we turn away from the worldly mindset of living for ourselves and just living life to the fullest, God rewards us for living fully for Him because these virtues are evidence of a life committed to bearing fruit and living fully for God.

Live God's Way

The right attitude for an impactful legacy is to live God's way. Galatians 5:22-23a says, "But what happens when we live God's way? He brings gifts into our lives, much the same way that fruit appears in an orchard—

things like affection for others, exuberance about life, serenity. We develop a willingness to stick with things, a sense of compassion in the heart, and a conviction that a basic holiness permeates things and people. We find ourselves involved in loyal commitments, not needing to force our way in life, able to marshal and direct our energies wisely" (MSG). By living God's way, our legacy will reflect the gifts God brought into our lives. Since we fulfilled God's plans for our life and His purpose for our legacy we will be remembered for our affection for others, our exuberance about life, and our serenity. We bring glory to God by directing our energies wisely, living fully for Him as we live His way.

Live With God's Word

The right attitude for an impactful legacy is to live in pursuit of a deeper faith by keeping God's Word in our hearts. God's Word was written to be studied, understood, and applied. When we spend time with God and study His Word, our actions and attitudes honor God as we study, understand and apply it. Reading the Bible helps you know God's Word, which is eternal truth and wisdom. When you read the Bible, you are feeding your soul with God's Word and putting God first before all things. The Bible promises we will find God when we search for Him with all our hearts and souls. Deuteronomy 4:29 promises, "But if from there you seek the Lord your God, you will find him if you seek him with all your heart and with all your soul" (NIV). The more we delight in God's presence, the more fruitful we are because our lives will reflect the fruits of the Spirit, love, joy, peace, patience, kindness, goodness, faithfulness, gentleness, and self-control as we keep God's Word in our hearts. Live with God's Word and your heart will reflect God's love and faithfulness and your legacy will reflect your heart.

Bible reading plans teach you how to read your Bible in one year. Devotional books highlight verses from the Bible which will help you get to know God on a daily basis. Living a legacy life enables us to find joy because our prayers and gratitude no longer change with our circumstances or feelings. Spending time in God's Word is important because when we are spending time reading the Bible, we know God. When we make a conscious decision to do what God says, we begin to see and serve people differently. When we do God's will, it is easier to be joyful and thankful in our current circumstances. Reading the Bible allows God to direct our steps so we no longer walk alone or without direction. But God can't direct our steps if we are not spending time in His Word so choose a reading plan or a devotional guide and start today.

Live A Truly Good Life

God is glorified when we live a truly good life. Living a truly good life is more than being honest and doing what is right. We are called to bear fruit and have an impact for God. John 15:8 reminds us, "When you produce much fruit, you are my true disciples. This brings great glory to my Father" (NLT). The same verse translated differently in the ERV says, "Show that you are my followers by producing much fruit. This will bring honor to my Father." Both translations show us when we bear fruit, we bring honor and glory to God. We bear fruit when we no longer seek to serve ourselves because we have a changed purpose. When we live out our legacy life with the purpose of bearing fruit, we have direction. When we have direction, we have an impact for God when we share our faith and let God love others through us. We are remembered for how we lived fully alive because our hearts reflect the real person God created us to be as we fulfilled His plans for our life and His purpose for our legacy to love Him and to love others.

Live By Prayer

The right attitude for an impactful legacy is to live by prayer and present our requests to God in every situation. One way to seek and know God is to spend time with Him in prayer. The Bible tells us how to know God and what living the Christian life looks like. God provides wisdom and discernment when we constantly communicate with God in prayer. Colossians 4:2-4 says that we should constantly pray and communicate with God so that he can provide us with wisdom and discernment. Our reward for spending time in prayer is to know God because He provides us with wisdom and discernment. It is this wisdom and discernment which ensures we live out the story God scripted specifically for us, because He reveals His plans when we know Him. When we know God and live out the story He scripted specifically for us, we are living fully for

Him and honoring Him with our legacy life. God gives us wisdom and victory when we live faithfully and keep our purpose in life clearly in mind instead of drifting through life. When we act responsibly with His gifts and resources He will guide us and reward our sincere and zealous efforts.

Philippians 4:6 reminds us, "Do not be anxious about anything, but in every situation, by prayer and petition, with thanksgiving, present your requests to God" (NIV). When we pray about every situation, there will be no room for our fear or anxious thoughts. Our attitude reflects our hearts when we are thankful and express our gratitude as we pray. When we ask God for help with every situation as He fulfills His plans for our life and His purpose for our legacy we don't have to worry about anything, we will be remembered for how our hearts reflected the person God created us to be.

Live With Intention

The right attitude for an impactful legacy is to live with intention and to be intentional with our words and prayers so they bring healing to our loved ones. Proverbs 12:18 warns us, "The words of the reckless pierce like swords, but the tongue of the wise brings healing" (NIV). Careless words cause more pain, not healing for broken and grieving hearts. To avoid being careless with our words, we must examine our hearts, since our hearts determine our speech. Author Jackie Hill Perry provides helpful insight on how our hearts determine our speech, "Someone might attempt to fix the problem of the tongue by simply refusing to talk, but silence doesn't regenerate or sanctify. To tame the tongue, we have to actually deal with who we are. 'Out of the abundance of the heart [the] mouth speaks' (Luke 6:45). By dealing with not just the words we say but also the heart that determines the speech, we can work toward the unity of our words and our worship."[36] Perry has an excellent point, we have to actually deal with who we are because what is in our hearts will come out in our speech and behavior. We will have an impactful legacy and glorify God when our hearts reflect the unity of our words and our worship and bring healing to our loved ones.

36 Perry, Jackie Hill. *Upon Waking.* Brentwood, TN. B&H Publishing Group, 2023, 46-47.

Live For Good

The right attitude for an impactful legacy is to live for good not evil. In this quote, Perry relies on Luke 6:45, "The good person out of the good treasure of his heart produces good, and the evil person out of his evil treasure produces evil, for out of the abundance of the heart his mouth speaks" (ESV). This verse reminds us our speech and actions reveal our true underlying beliefs, attitudes, and motivations. This verse is an excerpt from Jesus's teaching about fruit in people's lives. Jesus taught from the overflow of our heart, our mouth speaks. When our mouth speaks, our words embody our true underlying beliefs, attitudes, and motivations. When our attitude is focused on producing good, we will be remembered for how our hearts reflected the good person God created us to be and the fruit in our lives which reflected evidence of a life committed to bearing fruit and living fully for God.

Live With A Good Heart

The right attitude for an impactful legacy is to pay attention to what we are storing up in our hearts. Luke 6:45 says, "A good man brings good things out of the good stored up in his heart, and an evil man brings evil things out of the evil stored up in his heart. For the mouth speaks what the heart is full of" (NIV). This is why speaking from the heart is a reflection of our true underlying beliefs, attitudes, and motivations. If we want to be good and bring good things out of the good stored up in our hearts, we must store up good in our hearts. To store up good in our hearts, we must examine our hearts to ensure our beliefs, attitudes, and motivations are aligned with God's plan for our life and purpose for our legacy.

Live With A Heart For God

The right attitude for an impactful legacy is to put God first before all things in your life. Colossians 1:17 says, "He is before all things, and in him all things hold together" (NIV). Your legacy reflects your heart when you have a heart for God. Your heart is right with God when you put Him first before all things. By reading your Bible every day, God can speak to your heart and breathe life into every word. God teaches us His ways and His laws which enable us to do the right thing. Your sincere devotion of the heart is reflected in your daily schedule and how you are spending your time. Your heart is loyal to God when you actively choose to give God first place in every area of your life. When you give God first place in every area of your life, He will give you strength. 2 Chronicles 16:9 promises, "The Lord keeps close watch over the whole world, to give strength to those whose hearts are loyal to him" (GNT). When our hearts are loyal to God, He will reward us with His powerful strength and guidance to do the right thing as we fulfill His plans for our lives and His purpose for our legacy.

Love And Obey God

The right attitude for an impactful legacy is to love and obey Him first. God is pleased when we do what is right and just. Proverbs 21:3 reminds us, "To do what is right and just is more acceptable to the Lord than sacrifice" (NIV). To act justly is to do what is right and just. When our attitudes and behaviors please God, we bring Him glory. God doesn't want our gifts and sacrifices; He wants us to love and obey Him first. God can work in our lives when we acknowledge our sins and wicked ways so we can receive His forgiveness and guidance. God wants our hearts—our complete love and devotion. We must live by both love and justice and keep them in balance. We must love with justice so we don't excuse wrongdoing and keep people in their sins by failing to encourage them to a higher standard of righteousness. Love and justice are at the very foundation of God's character and we must find a perfect balance so we can be just with love or we will drive people away from God. For the sake of legacy, it's not too late to be more righteous and less wicked in our daily living. When we live fully for God and make every effort to glorify Him with our life and legacy He will give us everything we need. Matthew 6:33 promises, "Seek the Kingdom of God above all else, and live righteously, and he will give you everything you need" (NLT). The person we decide to be will affect every area of our lives and legacy. Proverbs 21:21 tells us, "Whoever pursues righteousness and love finds life, prosperity and honor" (NIV). Righteous people attain life because they live life more fully each day with a hopeful outlook on life as they experience the deep and everlasting love God has for them, a love which brings true peace and restoration.

Serve Each Other In Love

We are called to serve each other in love. Galatians 5:13 says, "You, my brothers and sisters, were called to be free. But do not use your freedom to indulge the flesh; rather, serve one another humbly in love" (NIV). When we serve each other, we are humbly serving others instead of ourselves. To fully understand Scripture, it is helpful to read more than one Bible translation. Galatians 5:13 says, "As for you, my friends, you were called to be free. But do not let this freedom become an excuse for letting your physical desires control you. Instead, let love make you serve one another" (GNT). This translation reminds us that it is love that motivates us to serve one another. I also find clarity when reading the Message translation. In studying this verse, we learn everything we know about God's Word is summed up in a single sentence. Galatians 5:13 says, "It is absolutely clear that God has called you to a free life. Just make sure that you don't use this freedom as an excuse to do whatever you want to do and destroy your freedom. Rather, use your freedom to serve one another in love; that's how freedom grows. ***For everything we know about God's Word is summed up in a single sentence: Love others as you love yourself.*** That's an act of true freedom. If you bite and ravage each other, watch out—in no time at all you will be annihilating each other, and where will your precious freedom be then?" (MSG, emphasis mine). The entire Bible, all that we know about God's Word, is a clear directive. To live fully and to bring God glory, all we must do is love others as we love ourselves. You achieve an extraordinary life and legacy when your heart reflects the real you, the person God created you to be so you can love others.

Scripture Prompt: "Study More!"

> "As a face is reflected in water, so the heart reflects the real person." —Proverbs 27:19 (NLT)

Prayer Prompt: "Pray Now!"

Dear Lord,

I commit my life and the time I have left investing in loving you and loving others so my heart will reflect your love and faithfulness. I want to live out the extraordinary life and legacy you created me for so I can bear fruit and live your way. Help me be a loving person by feeling loved and acting loyally and responsibly toward you and others. Show me how to be a faithful person and not only believe the truth but work for justice for others. Help me develop love and faithfulness as important character qualities so my actions and attitudes are aligned with your plans for my life and purpose for my legacy.

Amen

Writing Prompt: "Write Now!"

Journal and reflect about the fruit of the Spirit and the character traits found in the nature of Christ. Write about the qualities you want the Holy Spirit to produce in you so your heart reflects the real you, the person God created you to be. Write about the virtues you see in your life and the gifts God will bring into your life as you live God's way and leave an impactful legacy.

Worship Prompt: "Listen Now!"

"Holy Spirit" by Francesca Battistelli[37]

As you listen to these lyrics, rejoice and be glad God designed our hearts to long for His presence as He fills us with living hope. The song reminds us to seek His presence. As we become more aware of His presence, we can experience the glory of His goodness. When we experience the glory of His goodness, we experience peace of mind and peace of heart as we welcome the Holy Spirit into our minds and hearts. Then our hearts can reflect God's love and faithfulness.

37 Battistelli, Francesca. "Holy Spirit." *If We're Honest.* Written by Bryan Torwalt and Katie Torwalt. Word Entertainment and Fervent Records, 2014, https://francescamusic.com/.

Chapter Six

Eternal Perspective: Acknowledging Life Is Short, No Matter How Long You Live

When you acknowledge life is short, no matter how long you live you will have an eternal perspective and Godly wisdom. An eternal perspective helps us realize the true goal of life is to know God and the reward of life is to see God one day. When we recognize the brevity of life, we no longer disregard the sense of urgency and we take immediate action so we don't miss the opportunity to write legacy love letters to help our loved ones grieve differently.

God's Purposes Last Eternally

God's plans for your life and purpose for your legacy will never change because His plans endure forever and His purposes last eternally. Psalm 33:11 promises, "But his plans endure forever; his purposes last eternally" (GNT). This biblical promise reminds us our God is trustworthy because His intentions never change. Not only is God trustworthy, but God is also consistent because His love, His Word and His plans for your life and purpose for your legacy will never change. You can trust God with His plans for your life and purpose for your legacy because His plans endure forever, and His purposes last eternally.

A Heart Of Wisdom

Psalm 90:12 says, "Teach us to number our days, that we may gain a heart of wisdom" (NIV). Legacy love letter writers gain a heart of wisdom and come to terms with the brevity of life as they learn how to number their days. Some describe this verse by saying "no day is promised" or "life is short." When we learn to number our days, we gain a heart of wisdom which means we become wise. Legacy love letter writers become wise about how to use the limited time they have left. Their actions and behaviors prove they have come to terms with the biblical truth life is short and their days are numbered. They make a commitment to writing their legacy love letters before they run out of time. They set the goal of writing legacy letters to their loved ones. They make their goal a priority by scheduling a weekend retreat or attending an online course. With a heart of wisdom, they make every effort to help their loved ones grieve with the hope of heaven because they have received a legacy gift of love, faith, hope, and gratitude.

Author and publisher Brian Dixon has a heart of wisdom. As a young man he almost died in a car accident. This near death experience gave him a second chance at life and a heart for legacy. Since that day, he approaches life with this perspective, he says, "I have vision, make decisions, and take action based on my number of days."[38] In his latest

38 Dixon, Brian. "I have vision, make decisions, and take action based on my number of days." Facebook, 10 April. 2025, https://www.facebook.com/brianjdixon/posts/pfbid02o7dj4CZXqjoM1yKZMwPzDpxCoiPrcLCAEoZeBokAr F292hVgW9UoBWtkwNuE5WuTl.

book, *Your Hope Story: A Step-by-Step Guide to Help You Write and Publish Your First Book*, Brian teaches, "Writing your story leaves a legacy."[39] He believes that by writing and sharing your story you can help others. The writer's mindset to share your hope story is the same mindset needed to write legacy love letters. Brian asks, "What if you could send them a love letter?"[40] By sharing your life lessons in a letter or a book, you leave an impactful legacy that will help others for generations to come but you must have vision, make decisions, and take action based on your number of days.

The Gift Of God Is Eternal Life

The Bible promises Christians will inherit eternal life. Titus 3:7 promises, "Because of his grace he made us right in his sight and gave us confidence that we will inherit eternal life" (NLT). Romans 6:23 says, "For the wages of sin is death, but the gift of God is eternal life in Christ Jesus our Lord" (NIV). The gift of eternal life is a gift from God out of His love for us. We do not need to earn this gift. Just as we give gifts to our loved ones, we do not expect them to pay us back. We give to them out of our love and we expect only acceptance with gratitude. John 3:16 says, "For this is how God loved the world: He gave his one and only Son, so that everyone who believes in him will not perish but have eternal life" (NLT). Those who love Him will be rewarded with life forever in His presence. Our legacy letters comfort our loved ones with the hope of eternal life and help them overcome the challenge to continue living holy lives. Jesus Christ suffered for us and will carry us through everything. He showed us by example how to stand firm even when we are facing trials. We will still face trials here on earth but we will do so with living hope.

Keep Your Eyes On Eternity

When we keep our eyes on eternity, we can remain focused on what truly matters. 2 Corinthians 4:17 reminds us, "For our light and momentary

39 Dixon, Brian. *Your Hope*Story: A Step-by-Step Guide to Help You Write and Publish Your First Book.* Matthews, NC, hope*books, 2024, 4.

40 Dixon, 4.

troubles are achieving for us an eternal glory that far outweighs them all" (NIV). Reading further, 2 Corinthians 4:18 says, "So we fix our eyes not on what is seen, but on what is unseen, since what is seen is temporary, but what is unseen is eternal" (NIV). Keeping our eyes on eternity will help us fulfill God's plan for our lives and purpose for our legacy. When we stay focused on eternity, we have an eternal perspective and a heart for legacy. When our loved ones set their minds on things above, they can look at life from God's perspective and seek what He desires for their legacy.

Make Sure Each Day Counts

God has plans for our life and a purpose for our legacy, so it is no surprise we will be held responsible for how we live each day. We are only here on this earth for a short time, a dash. Each day is counted so each one of us needs to decide if we are just going to do our time by going through the motions of working, eating, and sleeping or if we are going to make sure each day counts by loving and living for God. If you are just going through the motions of working, eating, and sleeping then you are living half-dead. Sarah Mae says, "A fully alive people living for the living God can accomplish much in the world, but a half-dead people will just survive."[41] So stop living half-dead by going through the motions of working, eating, and sleeping. Start wanting something more out of your life and legacy than the daily grind by making sure each day counts by loving and living for God.

"Live Like You Were Dying!"

The phrase "Live like you were dying" was made popular by Tim McGraw's song, "Live Like You Were Dying."[42] The song tells the story of a man who received a life-threatening diagnosis. The activities he wanted to experience before he died were skydiving, mountain climbing,

41 Mae, Sarah. *Longing For Paris: One Woman's Search for Joy, Beauty, and Adventure—Right Where She Is.* Carol Stream, IL, Tyndale Momentum, 2015, 20.

42 McGraw, Tim. "Live Like You Were Dying." *Live Like You Were Dying.* Written by Craig Wiseman, Tim Nichols, and David Campbell. Curb Records, 2004. https://www.timmcgraw.com/.

fishing, and bull riding. This popular phrase may convince you to enjoy a final meal or final trip by completing an item on your bucket list. I don't have a bucket list in writing yet, but I know I have marked one item off the list already. My whole life, I dreamed of ice skating in New York City at Rockefeller Center under the Christmas tree. I had the chance to fulfill this dream the year my son was a freshman in high school. He wanted to see New York City and I wanted to ice skate, so we took the trip. This was a memorable trip for both of us and I will always cherish the memories. We still joke about our last night in the city when I ordered two pizzas instead of two slices of pizza. When the order arrived at our hotel, the New York style pizza was so large each slice filled an entire plate. I had mistakenly ordered too much food. The trip was special to me because skating in New York on the Rockefeller rink was a dream I had held in my heart since I was a little girl seeing it on TV. The trip to fulfill this wish was even better since I made the memory with my son. This great experience was definitely a bucket list item, an activity I wanted to experience before I died.

Create A Bucket List And Create A Specific Timeline

A bucket list is an itemized list of goals people want to accomplish before they die, or "kick the bucket." Even though I don't have one in writing yet, I think bucket lists are helpful because they motivate people to accomplish certain things within a specific timeline. If you want help creating your own bucket list, I suggest you visit the website: https://med.stanford.edu/letter/bucket-list.html. Stanford Medicine's Healthy Aging lab has created this resource because they discovered bucket lists serve as a roadmap and help doctors provide personalized care. They found many people have health-related goals on their bucket list and when they share their goals with their doctor, their doctor can help them. I recommend using a bucket list approach for legacy planning if it motivates you to accomplish it within a specific timeline.

A Bucket List Recognizes Mortality

"What is the symbolic meaning of a bucket list?" asks V.J. Periyakoil then explains, "It is a tangible recognition of our mortality. It allows us to reflect on what matters most to us, on our personal values and identify important life milestones and experiences that we want to have before a certain milestone in our life (e.g. high school graduation, college graduation, before retirement, before we die)."[43] I agree with the author's explanation that a bucket list is symbolic as the list maker recognizes their mortality. I have found in my law practice that my clients usually come to me to put their legal affairs in order because they have just experienced the loss of a loved one or they are faced with a diagnosis of a terminal illness or an emergency surgery. When people are in the season of legacy planning, they are putting their affairs in order, they are reflecting on what matters most and they are recognizing their mortality. It is this recognition of mortality which allows them to seek God's eternal perspective and His heart for legacy.

Seek Godly Wisdom

Even though God is the author of your story, it's up to you to seek God's eternal perspective to receive godly wisdom. James 1:5 teaches us, "If any of you lacks wisdom, you should ask God, who gives generously to all without finding fault, and it will be given to you" (NIV). This is a prayer God answers generously. Simply ask God for wisdom. Just pray, "Give me wisdom and an eternal perspective." Do not complicate your request, it can be this short prayer. You do have a say and a part to play in what your future and your legacy look like. Wise people seek God's eternal perspective. Wisdom is the ability to make wise decisions in difficult circumstances. Whenever you need wisdom, you can pray to God, and He will generously supply what you need. God will fill your life with purpose and meaning as you seek God's eternal perspective. Ask God to reveal His truth to you and you'll experience His deep love, His promises, and His plan for your life and purpose for your legacy. Godly wisdom will guide your journey by nourishing your soul each day as well as correct and convict you when needed.

43 Stanford Medicine. "I Matter Too: What is a Bucket List?" *Letter Project*, Stanford University School of Medicine, https://med.stanford.edu/letter/bucket-list/what-is-bucket-list.html.

To Take To Heart

Pastor Ted Cunningham starts every funeral the same way—with Ecclesiastes 7:1-2, "A good name is better than fine perfume, and the day of death better than the day of birth. It is better to go to a house of mourning than to go to a house of feasting, for death is the destiny of everyone; the living should take this to heart" (NIV). When speaking on a Focus on The Family broadcast, he told the story of preaching at his father-in-law's funeral. He said, "Today, we're here to take to heart the death of Lloyd Freitag. And the scripture says it's better to go to a funeral than to go to a party, and the reason for that is because a funeral is a recalibrating event. A funeral should change the way you think and it should change the way you live. I don't get that at a party. I don't walk away from a party ever going, 'Well, that changed my life. It was good fellowship. It was good medicine as we laughed together.'"[44] Pastor Ted's advice is godly wisdom because it shows us how to have an eternal perspective. He reminds us a funeral, not a party, is a recalibrating event. To have a heart of wisdom, you have an eternal perspective, and you are changing the way you think and live. When you have a heart of wisdom and live a life with an eternal perspective, you too will hear them say, "Today, we're here to take to heart the death of ________."

Scripture Prompt: "Study More!"

> "Teach us to number our days, that we may gain a heart of wisdom." —Psalm 90:12 (NIV).

Prayer Prompt: "Pray Now!"

Dear Lord,

Thank you for creating me as a work of art and designing this legacy life specifically for me so I leave an impactful legacy. Help me live each day with an eternal perspective no matter how long I live so I gain a heart of wisdom

44 "Encouraging Marriages in Your Sphere of Influence." *Focus on the Family with Jim Daly*, 9 August 2024, https://www.focusonthefamily.com/episodes/broadcast/encouraging-marriages-in-your-sphere-of-influence/.

and have vision, make decisions, and take action so your wondrous works are remembered.

Amen

Writing Prompt: "Write Now!"

All our stories are impacted by somebody we lost at a young age or an old age. Journal and reflect about life being short no matter how long you live. Write about what decisions and actions you will take now to leave a legacy with maximum impact. Consider Pastor Ted Cunningham's advice about a funeral being a recalibrating event. Do you believe a funeral should change the way you think and the way you live?

Worship Prompt: "Listen Now!"

"Living Hope" by Phil Wickham[45]

This song includes the powerful lyric, "Hallelujah, death has lost its grip on me."[46] The song inspires us to rely on God for living hope. Because death has lost its grip on us, we can praise God. Jesus died for our sins to set us free. I still remember hearing these powerful lyrics in person at a Phil Wickham concert in Stockton, California. I have been a business sponsor of KYCC radio for years and I attended the concert with all three of my children. We entered the church and found our seats, but it was no ordinary church worship service. We worshiped together and bought a CD to take home. This song brings back the special memory of that night. When we celebrate God's victory over death we can sing with confidence, "Hallelujah, death has lost its grip on me." This biblical truth sets us free from the lies of the enemy who tells us death is the end of the story. We can live a life of freedom as we live each day with living hope. We can live each day with an eternal perspective as we gain a heart of wisdom and have vision, make decisions, and take action so that His wondrous works are remembered.

45 Wickham, Phil. "Living Hope." *Living Hope.* Written by Phil Wickham and Brian Johnson. Fair Trade Services, 2018, https://philwickham.com/.

46 Wickham.

Chapter Seven

Alert Mind: Living A Legacy Life Requires God's Wisdom and Discernment

Living a legacy life that makes an impact for God requires an Alert mind. An alert mind is a sound mind. To obtain and maintain an alert mind, you must seek God's wisdom and discernment in everything you do. Then you will see clearly God's plan for your life and purpose for your legacy despite a chaotic and noisy world.

An Alert Mind Recognize The Voice Of The Enemy Speaking Lies

Let God transform you by changing the way you think and by helping you recognize the voice of the enemy speaking lies. God's wisdom and discernment will help you take control of your mind and emotions.

Then you will have the discernment to recognize the voice of the enemy speaking lies. God can take away all deception so you will not accept a lie for truth. With God's wisdom and discernment, you can live a legacy life by clearly recognizing the enemy's deception. Satan's only purpose is to destroy your life so your legacy does not have the full impact God designed. When you recognize the deception, you can replace the lies you are believing with the truth. For an alert mind, ask God for help to fill your mind with the truth and thoughts that are pleasing to Him. Trust God to give you the wisdom, discernment, and strength to resist filling your mind with anything not from Him or that does not bring Him glory.

Let God Renew Your Mind

A sound mind is a mind renewed, so let God transform you by changing the way you think. Romans 12:2 says, "Don't copy the behavior and customs of this world, but let God transform you into a new person by changing the way you think. Then you will learn to know God's will for you, which is good and pleasing and perfect" (NLT). Change the way you think by filling your mind with thoughts that please God. In prayer, take all your worries, fears, and doubts to the Lord. Ask God to give you the spirit of discernment to keep your thoughts and feelings focused on Him. God will change the way you think when you stop, pray and ask God to help you focus on what is true.

Fill Your Mind With Thoughts That Please God

To fill your mind with thoughts that please God, think about things that are true, noble, just, pure, lovely, good, virtuous, and praiseworthy. Philippians 4:8 says, "Finally, brothers and sisters, whatever is true, whatever is noble, whatever is right, whatever is pure, whatever is lovely, whatever is admirable—if anything is excellent or praiseworthy—think about such things" (NIV). By filling your mind with thoughts that please God you are changing the way you think and you will have an alert and sound mind which will help you live a legacy life with full impact.

Excellent And Worthy Of Praise

To ensure a sound mind, think about things that are excellent and worthy of praise. Philippians 4:8-9 says, "Summing it all up, friends, I'd say you'll do best by filling your minds and meditating on things true, noble, reputable, authentic, compelling, gracious—the best, not the worst; the beautiful, not the ugly; things to praise, not things to curse. Put into practice what you learned from me, what you heard and saw and realized. Do that, and God, who makes everything work together, will work you into his most excellent harmonies" (MSG). This paraphrase of the verse provides three steps to maintain a sound mind. First, focus on the best, not the worst. Next, focus on the beautiful, not the ugly. Then focus on things to praise, not to curse. Use these three steps as you breathe in truth and breathe out the lies of the enemy. As you replace each lie with the truth, the truth will set you free. You will be free from the enemy's deception as you put into practice what you learned. When you are truly free, God will use you in extraordinary ways.

Meditate On Things That Are Best

These three steps demonstrate how we can ensure an alert and sound mind for ourselves and for our loved ones. I appreciate The Message Bible paraphrase of Philippians 4:8-9 because it shows us practical examples of how to fill our minds and to meditate on things that are best, not the worst; the beautiful, not the ugly; things to praise, not things to curse. When we meditate on things that are the best, the beautiful, and worthy of praise we will ensure a sound mind for ourselves as we take every thought captive and make it obedient to Christ. As 2 Corinthians 10:5 reminds us, we must "take captive every thought to make it obedient to Christ" (NIV). When we have an alert and sound mind, we can show our loved ones how they can meditate on things that are best, beautiful, and worthy of praise.

Estate Planning Requires A Sound Mind

God promises us a sound mind. A sound mind is clear, alert, bright, intelligent, stable, peaceful, and uncluttered. Estate planning requires a sound mind. Estate attorneys follow best practices and procedures to ensure proper execution of the legal documents that make up an estate plan because if the document is invalid it has no legal effect and can be thrown out of court. To prove a valid will in California, a witness must sign and be prepared to testify under penalty of perjury, "***We understand this instrument to be the testator's Last Will and Testament. The testator thereupon signed this Last Will and Testament in our presence, all of us being present at the same time. To the best of our knowledge, the testator was at the time eighteen (18) years or older, of sound mind, and under no constraint or undue influence. We now, at the testator's request, in the testator's presence and in the presence of each other, subscribe our names as witnesses.***" This witness declaration in California is an important part of the signing process and offers some comic relief to a serious meeting. Most often than not my client will laugh out loud and even make a comment or a joke about whether they are of sound mind. We all laugh out loud because we live in a chaotic and noisy world. We know we are always under a lot of influence, especially due to stress and worry over our relationships and our health and our finances. As an estate attorney, I must be ready to testify that my client has sufficient mental capacity to be able to understand the nature of the testamentary act, understand and recollect the nature and situation of the individual's property, and remember and understand the individual's relations to living descendants, spouse, and parents, and those whose interests are affected by the will. This is the legal version; a simpler version of this requirement is to say I must be ready to testify that my client knows who they are and what they have to give to their beneficiaries.

A Weakened State Of Mind

Even someone with a diagnosis of Alzheimer's disease can still sign their last will and testament if at the moment of signing they had capacity and knew who they were and what they owned. Unfortunately, in court there are a number of elder abuse cases because somebody is taking advantage of an individual with a weakened state of mind. One elder abuse case I argued in court involved an individual who suffered from a weakened state of mind as the result of Alzheimer's. The parties did settle the case before the end of the trial but before the settlement, each party presented their witnesses so the judge could determine whether the defendant was guilty of elder abuse. In California, if a defendant is found guilty of elder abuse, then the defendant is deemed to have predeceased the decedent. This means the defendant does not receive an inheritance so justice can prevail. In this case, the decedent's valid will devised her estate to be shared equally between her two children. But during her weakened state of mind as the result of Alzheimer's disease, her son had caused the Grant Deed to be drafted and the decedent to sign it even though it was contrary to her original instructions contained in her will. The decedent's son caused the Grant Deed to be recorded in the County Recorder's Office. The complaint for elder abuse presented to the judge proved the decedent lacked capacity to convey her real property to her son and she lacked capacity to understand the conveyance was contrary to her original instructions contained in her will, which devised her estate to be shared equally between her two children. At the time the defendant caused the decedent to execute the Grant Deed at issue, the decedent was substantially unable to manage her own financial resources or resist undue influence and was otherwise of unsound mind, because she suffered from advanced Alzheimer's Disease.

A Strong Mind

In another case I was involved in, there was a will contest based on lack of capacity. The decedent was a terminally ill cancer patient who signed a will ten days before he died. At the time he signed his will, he was heavily medicated and in hospice care. Witnesses were ready to testify he seemed out of it and unable to carry on a conversation other than basic salutations. In presenting the case for lack of capacity, evidence proved his terminal illness made him physically and mentally weak. To have capacity, one must be strong physically and mentally. God's wisdom provides strength physically and mentally so we have the capacity we need.

An Alert Mind Sees Clearly And Hears Perfectly

The inability to see clearly or hear perfectly prevents someone from having a complete understanding of what is in front of them. In a separate case, the validity of the document was questioned when I presented evidence to the judge that the decedent was legally blind and hard of hearing at the time of signing a last-minute modification to her trust, which made an unequal distribution to her children. To have an alert mind and a complete understanding of what is in front of them, one must see clearly and hear perfectly. This case example shows how important it is for each one of us to have an alert mind. If we cannot see clearly or hear perfectly, we must stop and pay attention and ask for help so we can obtain an alert mind and a complete understanding of what is in front of us. It reminds me of my Kindergarten teacher saying, "Stop, look, and listen." This is good advice for anyone struggling with seeing clearly or hearing perfectly. Just as we did in Kindergarten, stop what you are doing and pay attention. Then look and listen so you can see clearly and hear perfectly. For an alert mind and complete understanding be sure to, "Stop, look, and listen." Then ask God for the wisdom and discernment you need to live a legacy life that makes an impact for God.

Scripture Prompt: "Study More!"

> "Finally, brothers and sisters, whatever is true, whatever is noble, whatever is right, whatever is pure, whatever is lovely, whatever is admirable—if anything is excellent or praiseworthy—think about such things."
> —Philippians 4:8 (NIV)

Prayer Prompt: "Pray Now!"

Dear Lord,

Thank you for your gift of an alert and sound mind. Help me put into practice what I've learned from you and what I've heard, seen, and realized. I will continue to seek your wisdom and discernment in everything I do so I can live a legacy life which makes an impact for you and brings you glory. Please continue to fill my mind and help me meditate on whatever is true, noble, right, pure, lovely and admirable.

Amen

Writing Prompt: "Write Now!"

Journal and reflect about God's gift of a sound and alert mind. Write about things in your life that are excellent and worthy of praise so you can fill your mind and meditate on the best things, not the worst; the beautiful, not the ugly; and things to praise, not things to curse.

Worship Prompt: "Listen Now!"

"Sound Mind" by Melissa Helser[47]

This song boldly proclaims our inheritance of a sound mind. Melissa Helser reminds us we can see clearly with a sound mind. She sings about God walking with us and His presence when we are suffering. This worship song reminds us to remember who God is and to stand in His authority. When we stand in God's authority, His wisdom and discernment give us an alert mind so we can live the legacy life He designed specifically for us.

47 Melissa Helser. "Sound Mind." *The Land I'm Livin' In*. Written by Bryan Torwalt, Katie Torwalt, Melissa Helser, and Johathan David Helser. Bethel Music, 2022.

Chapter Eight

Legacy Heart: Loving And Living For God With Purpose

A legacy heart is a heart that loves and lives for God with purpose. When God created each one of us as a work of ART, He designed each one of us with a heart for legacy. When we love and live for God with purpose, we find contentment in His love and in doing His will. When God has changed our hearts for legacy, we turn toward God and rely on biblical guidance to find answers to our questions. Micah 6:8 answers the question, "What does God require of me?" Micah 6:8 says, "He has shown you, O mortal, what is good. And what does the Lord require of you? To act justly and to love mercy and to walk humbly with your God" (NIV).

It is helpful to consider another translation of this verse to further explore the answers God is writing on your mind and heart as you love and live for God with purpose. The Message translation simplifies the directive, "But he's already made it plain how to live, what to do, what God is looking for in men and women. It's quite simple: Do what is fair and just to your neighbor, be compassionate and loyal in your love, And don't take yourself too seriously—take God seriously" (Micah 6:8, MSG). This translation resonates with me because it reminds me I don't have to take myself too seriously. Instead, I will take God seriously as I simply love God and love people. As you love and live for God with purpose, have faith and confidence God will lead you as you trust Him to walk through each chapter of your legacy story and remember His promise He will see to it that everything works out for the best.

Do What Is Fair: Live And Love

To do what is fair is to live and love. As you live out your legacy story, you are an example to all in what you say in the way you live and love. 1 Timothy 4:12 tells us, "Let no one despise you for your youth, but set the believers an example in speech, in conduct, in love, in faith, in purity" (ESV). The Message translation adds more depth to this verse by suggesting it is not just how we live and love but how we use our special gift of ministry. 1 Timothy 4:11-14 says, "Get the word out. Teach all these things. And don't let anyone put you down because you're young. Teach believers with your life: by word, by demeanor, by love, by faith, by integrity. Stay at your post reading Scripture, giving counsel, teaching. And that special gift of ministry you were given when the leaders of the church laid hands on you and prayed—keep that dusted off and in use" (MSG). This translation encourages believers to make an impact for God by bringing more people to Heaven. We are encouraged to teach believers with spoken and written words. Our patience and kindness is reflected in our actions and attitudes which honor God. Our life speaks and teaches believers we love God and love others. We teach believers with our life as we love God; know God; trust God; obey God; and serve God. Believers see our faith when we keep our promises and apologize for our mistakes. Let us do what is fair so we not only get to Heaven but we take our loved ones with us. God has already made it plain how to live and love, to leave a legacy that glorifies Him.

Be Compassionate And Loyal In Your Love

To be compassionate and loyal in your love requires your whole heart for legacy. God wants your whole heart. To give God your whole heart, you can pray this short prayer, "Forgive me and make my heart right with you." God wants to forgive our sins and restore our relationship with Him. God mends our relationship and gives us a clean heart. Psalm 51:10 shows us how to pray, "Create in me a pure heart, O God, and renew a steadfast spirit within me" (NIV). Extraordinary living leaves an extraordinary legacy, but to live fully alive for God's glory requires a heart for legacy. So be compassionate and loyal in your love and give God your whole heart so he can restore the joy of your salvation. God wants to help you rebuild your life as He creates a pure heart and spirit in you. Many psalms are intense prayers asking God for forgiveness. Pray Psalm 51:12, "Restore to me the joy of your salvation and grant me a willing spirit, to sustain me" (NIV). We can honestly pray directly to God because He forgives us. When we confess our sin and turn from it, we receive forgiveness and love. The more you feel God's everlasting love and forgiveness, the more you will tell your loved ones about it. God wants us all to be close to Him so we can experience the joy of His salvation and a clean heart and spirit. God will create a pure heart and spirit in you so you can be compassionate and loyal in your love. So you can love and live for God with purpose.

Let God Be The Strength Of Your Legacy Heart

Psalm 73:26 reminds us to let God be the strength of our hearts, "My flesh and my heart may fail, but God is the strength of my heart and my portion forever" (NIV). Failure is an ongoing reality, not just a one-time event because we will face difficulties, failure and hardship on this side of Heaven. You can grow from your biggest failures and your smallest mistakes so let God be the strength of your legacy heart. Our Heavenly Father loves us so much He has created each one of us with a heart for legacy. The word "forever" reminds us to live each day with an eternal perspective, since our relationship with God is of an eternal nature when compared to the temporary nature of human life. The treasures in heaven God promises us are of eternal value.

Everything Works Together For The Good

Not only will God be the strength of our hearts, He causes everything to work together for the good of those who love Him. Romans 8:28 tells us, "And we know that God causes everything to work together for the good of those who love God and are called according to his purpose for them" (NLT). When considering what your last words to those you love will be, you should consider including this verse. Author Zig Ziglar included this verse in his last written words to his son Tom Ziglar who shared them as a foreword to his book, *Choose To Win.* Despite his struggle with Alzheimer's, Zig Ziglar wrote, "For my son who I love and am very proud and grateful for. Romans 8:28."[48] Tom shares that his parents left a legacy by design, based on the intentional choices they made. He teaches his audience that significance and legacy are intentional and give meaning and purpose to your life.[49]

Walk Humbly

Micah 6:8 reminds us to walk humbly with God. As you Walk Humbly With God, turn toward God for His strength and let Him help you grow through your small mistakes and your big failures so you will become wiser. Let your happiness and hope come from building a life based on faith and having confidence in God's presence and guidance. When you walk humbly with God, you can leave the world behind. When you leave the world behind, you are turning away from sin, temptation, violence, hurt, and pain. When you walk humbly with God, you know God and have a relationship with Him. When you have a relationship with God He will provide wisdom and discernment as He directs your steps. The more you walk humbly with God, you can love and live for God with purpose and find contentment in His love and in doing His will.

48 Ziglar, Tom. *Choose To Win: Transform Your Life One Simple Choice At A Time.* Nashville, TN, Nelson Books, 2019, vii.

49 Ziglar, vii.

Act Justly And Make Him Known

Until we are called home to Heaven, our life mission is to know God and make Him known. We know God by having a relationship with Him and by living a legacy life in pursuit of a deeper faith. We make Him known by leading others to a relationship with Christ so they too can spend eternity in Heaven. When we lead others to a relationship with Christ, we are living a meaningful legacy life because we will be remembered for how we loved them with our words and actions. This legacy brings glory to God, who created us to have an impact and to be remembered.

Ordinary And Extraordinary

To have an impact and to be remembered illustrates the difference between ordinary and extraordinary. I have known this term throughout my law career; in the probate court I can petition the court for additional fees if I can prove to the judge my work qualifies for extraordinary service. When I counsel clients who are performing in their roles as executors or trustees, they have a number of duties to perform to fulfill their obligations under the law. When either the attorney or the executor perform extraordinary services, it is beyond what is required by law. Extraordinary is to do more than ordinary and more than what is expected.

Start Living An Extraordinary Life For Christ

Pastor Jeff Simmons wrote the book *Finding the Extra in Ordinary: Embracing the Beauty of the Christian Life.* He encourages his readers to live in the promises of God not in fear and worry because fear is one of the biggest deterrents to truly living an extraordinary life.[50] He explains, "An extraordinary life is lived by faith, not fear."[51] Simmons defines an ordinary existence as one consisting of predictable schedules, easily attainable goals, and reasonable expectations which leads to getting stuck in a life that lacks meaning, purpose, and joy. He teaches, "When you

50 Simmons, Jeff. *Finding the Extra in Ordinary: Embracing the Beauty of the Christian Life.* Carol Spring, IL, Tyndale House Publishers, 2024, 177.

51 Simmons, 187.

live your extraordinary life, you can impact generations to come."[52] The reward for living an extraordinary life for Christ is to have influence far beyond just you because it makes a difference in your church, workplace, community, and marriage which impacts your children, your grandchildren, and countless generations for the glory of God.[53]

Don't Lose Sight Of What God Says About You

We are deeply loved by a God who handcrafted us, shaped us, and formed us before we were born. We can improve our daily lives by refusing to get stuck in a life that lacks meaning, purpose, and joy. Don't lose sight of what God says about you and why He brought you into this world. God has a purpose specifically for you. He has created you not just to live life to the fullest, but to glorify Him by living fully. Simmons teaches his readers how to improve their daily lives, "You don't need to buy into the cultural norm of living an overcrowded and overscheduled existence."[54] He reminds them, "Freedom comes when you prioritize time with God, family, and close friends, plus a bit of margin in your schedule so that God can use you."[55] When you leave a margin in your schedule, God can use you to live an extraordinary life for Christ. Simmons says, "Many people live passive lives, yet Jesus invites us to get involved and make a difference in the lives of others."[56] Don't lose sight of what God says about you, he created you to make the difference in the lives of others.

Be Known For The Difference You Made For People

If your goal is to leave an impactful legacy, it will be the result of the investment you made in people. In *Start With Your People: The Daily Decision that Changes Everything,* author Brian Dixon recounts attending a funeral service. "As the service progressed, through stories, songs and prayers, I clearly saw the culmination of life. No one mentioned her

52 Simmons, 226.

53 Simmons, 222.

54 Simmons, 97.

55 Simmons, 97.

56 Simmons, 94.

worldly possessions or what she was leaving behind. Instead, everyone remembered the difference she made for people."[57] He concluded, "We spend so much time living our lives yet so little time designing our legacy. When our life is over, there's very little that will live on after us. When we really get down to it, our main legacy will be the investment we made in people."[58] He thought of Marie's funeral, the life she lived, the people she impacted, and the legacy she left. He encouraged his readers to consider their lasting legacy will be reflected in their level of engagement with those around them. He concluded, "One day, your people will gather to honor your life. To say goodbye and to recount the memories of times you shared with them. What do you want them to say? How do you want to be remembered? Your actions in the present influence their words in the future."[59] When you are remembered, it is because you made an impact on the world. Your life had a meaning and a purpose because you made a difference. Consider your relationships and how you are engaging with the people God has placed in your life. Spend time designing your legacy so your loved ones remember you for the difference you made for them.

Famous To One

When encouraging her readers not to be too concerned with impressing people here on Earth, author Kendra Roehl writes, "When we remember that as believers, we want nothing more than to hear God say, 'Well done,' we'll be faithful to do what he asks of us rather than worrying about what others may say or think. And when we're faithful to handle the small things that come our way, he'll give us even more responsibility—increasing our witness and influence with those around us."[60] She emphasizes Matthew 25:23, "The master said, 'Well done, my good and faithful servant. You have been faithful in handling this small amount, so now I will give you

57 Dixon, Brian, *Start With Your People: The Daily Decision that Changes Everything.* Grand Rapids, MI. Zondervan, 2019, 31.

58 Dixon, *Start With Your People: The Daily Decision that Changes Everything,* 30-31.

59 Dixon, *Start With Your People: The Daily Decision that Changes Everything,* 34-35.

60 Fisk, Julie, et al. *The One Year Daily Acts of Gratitude Devotional: 365 Inspirations to Encourage a Life of Thankfulness.* Carol Stream, IL, Tyndale Momentum, 2023, 151.

many more responsibilities. Let's celebrate together!'" (NLT). Her tattoo says, "Famous to One" because "being famous to Jesus is her ultimate goal in life." What she wants more than anything is to please Jesus in the way she loves Him, loves others, and shares His kindness with the world. She hopes when she gets to Heaven, Jesus will hug her and say, "I know you." Her statements resonated with me because I realized for a majority of my life, I was aiming to please people instead of aiming to be "famous to one." Consider adopting Kendra's ultimate goal in life, instead of being concerned about impressing people here on Earth, let your greatest desire be Jesus knows who you are and is proud of you. You can encourage your loved ones with this goal and write, "Remember, the ultimate goal in the Christian life is to be famous to one. I pray you are known for being faithful, rather than worrying about what others may say or think."

Place Your Ordinary Life Before God

Place your ordinary life before God as an offering. The Message version encourages us to fix our attention on God so he can bring the best out of us. Romans 12:1-2 says,

> So here's what I want you to do, God helping you: Take your everyday, ordinary life—your sleeping, eating, going-to-work, and walking-around life—and place it before God as an offering. Embracing what God does for you is the best thing you can do for him. Don't become so well-adjusted to your culture that you fit into it without even thinking. Instead, fix your attention on God. You'll be changed from the inside out. Readily recognize what he wants from you, and quickly respond to it. Unlike the culture around you, always dragging you down to its level of immaturity, God brings the best out of you, develops well-formed maturity in you. (MSG)

Your life is ordinary as you sleep, eat, go to work and walk around. When you focus your attention on God, He will change you from the inside out. You will no longer be satisfied living an ordinary life for yourself. Instead, God will bring the best out of you so you can fulfill His plans for your life and His purpose for your legacy.

Scripture Prompt: "Study More!"

> "He has shown you, O mortal, what is good. And what does the Lord require of you? To act justly and to love mercy and to walk humbly with your God." —Micah 6:8 (NIV)

Prayer Prompt: "Pray Now!"

Dear Lord,

Thank you for showing us what you require of us. We want to act justly, love mercy and walk humbly with you. Thank you for inviting us to walk with you and be in a relationship with you so you can provide wisdom and discernment. Help us love you and love others as we start living the extraordinary life you have for us. May our lives be an offering of love, bringing glory to your name! As we love mercy, help us demonstrate your love in words so love remains and we are remembered for the difference we made for people. As we act justly, help us demonstrate your love in actions and really love them.

Amen

Writing Prompt: "Write Now!"

Journal and reflect about the difference between an ordinary and an extraordinary life. Write about the risk of getting stuck in a life that lacks meaning, purpose, and joy. Think about what God has for you. What do you need to do to safeguard your life so you don't get stuck in a life that lacks meaning, purpose, and joy? What advice would you give your loved ones so they can live a life with meaning, purpose and joy? Will your legacy be the investment you made in people? What action will you take now to spend time designing your legacy so your loved ones remember you for the difference you made for them?

Worship Prompt: "Listen Now!"

"Act Justly, Love Mercy, Walk Humbly" by Pat Barrett[61]

This worship song reminds us life comes down to this: what God requires of us. As we sing along, we are encouraged to act justly, love mercy, and walk humbly with God in all things and all ways. The song encourages us to trade beauty for ashes and mourning for dancing so we can live knowing the truth that the Kingdom of Heaven is closer and closer. We can love and live for God with purpose since we know what God requires of us. God will be the strength of our legacy heart as we walk humbly in relationship with Him. We will live an extraordinary life as we live by faith, not fear. We will refuse to get stuck in a life that lacks meaning, purpose, and joy. We will engage with those around us so we will be remembered for the difference we made for people.

61 Barrett, Pat. "Act Justly, Love Mercy, Walk Humbly." *Act Justly, Love Mercy, Walk Humbly.* Composed by Pat Barrett, Jason Ingram, and Chris Tomlin. Sparrow Records, Bowyer & Bow, 2021, https://www.patbarrettmusic.com/.

PART THREE

HOW TO LEAVE A LASTING LEGACY: WRITE LETTERS

"Let all that you do be done in love."
—1 Corinthians 16:14, ESV

Chapter Nine

Speak TRUTH in Love: With Faith and Confidence Express Love

God created a masterpiece, a work of ART when he created you to speak Truth in Love. You will leave a lasting legacy that glorifies God when you speak Truth in love with faith and confidence as you express love to your loved ones. This part of the book identifies seven ingredients found in legacy love letters: love, faith, hope, gratitude, forgiveness, encouragement, and sympathy. You will learn how to leave a lasting legacy by writing love letters. Each letter in the acrostic TRUTH represents God's plans for your life and His purpose for your legacy to express love and demonstrate God's love in words and actions, that you *T—Trust God and express faith; R—Really love them and express forgiveness, help them become U—Unstoppable and express encouragement, be T—Thankful and express Gratitude, and leave a legacy gift of H—Hope and express hope* and *sympathy.*

God Is Love

Love is a commitment. If you commit to loving others, then you will stay one in your heart with God, and He'll stay one with you—because God is love. 1 John 4:16 says, "God is love. If we keep on loving others, we will stay one in our hearts with God, and he will stay one with us" (CEV). Your relationship with God is greatly affected by your relationship with other people. God's purpose for your legacy is to commit to expressing love and demonstrating God's love in words and actions. The reward for your commitment to love God and others will be a deeper faith and a more meaningful life.

Love, The Key Ingredient Of Any Love Letter

1 John 4:19 says, "We love because he first loved us" (ESV). A legacy with an everlasting impact is built with an unfailing love. In love we seek to love others as completely as God loves us. Your legacy love letter starts and ends with love, the key ingredient of any love letter. You leave an extraordinary legacy by loving God and loving others. In life and in death, we must give each other love and support. Love is the greatest of human qualities and is an attribute of God Himself because God is love.

Speak Truth

As followers of Christ, it is our duty to share the good news with the world. When we share our faith, we boldly proclaim the good news of the gospel. We make an impact for Christ as we speak truth. Sharing the good news and preaching the Word of God allows us to know how to do Christ's work on this side of Heaven. We have been given this important responsibility to take a stand for Christ and to tell our loved ones about His love and truth. When we speak truth to our loved ones, we can correct, rebuke, and encourage with great patience and careful instruction. 2 Timothy 4:2 reminds us, "Preach the word; be prepared in season and out of season; correct, rebuke and encourage—with great patience and careful instruction" (NIV). When we preach and teach we are making known the Word of God.

Speak Life

Your words have the power to speak life and to encourage your loved ones. The Bible guides us to speak the truth in love. This sounds simple, but it is hard for us to do. Ephesians 4:15 directs us, "Instead, speaking the truth in love, we will grow to become in every respect the mature body of him who is the head, that is, Christ" (NIV). The instruction here is to do both. For a lasting impact, we must speak truth and do it in a loving manner. Speaking the truth in love is required in all things, both our speech and our lives expressing His truth. We have the responsibility to steward what we are speaking and what we are writing in our legacy love letters. Your final words should be honest but be careful not to write words which will have a negative impact or will be read as criticism or rejection. Words spoken in anger, judgment or haste don't result in the same lasting impact as words spoken in love.

Don't Leave Anything Unsaid

Say your final goodbye with love and don't leave anything unsaid, especially your final "I love you." Upon your passing, your loved ones will pause to reflect and remember you, your character, and how you loved them. Memories will help them think about the love and care you showed to them and the time you spent with them on this side of Heaven. Your final words will have staying power because they were written with a life overflowing with purpose and love. When you are remembered, God's wondrous works are remembered. Your life had a purpose, and your legacy of love remains. Author Bob Goff, a former lawyer, says he used to devote way more time and energy to being a lawyer but then two things hit him one day: "First, all we'll leave behind is our love, and second, our legacy will be in the people we loved."[62] Our final goodbyes must be said with love because the love we leave behind will be our legacy. This quote resonated with me because it reminds me of what my life was like before I

62 Goff, Bob. *Live in Grace, Walk In Love: A 365-Day Journey.* Nashville, TN, Nelson Books, 2019, 61.

was laid off from my job as a corporate lawyer in San Diego. Even though I was earning a six-figure salary and big benefits, I was devoting way too much time and energy to being a lawyer. When we realize all we leave behind is our love and our legacy will be in the people we loved, we can devote our time and energy on living a life overflowing with purpose and love. I still devote a lot of time and energy to being a lawyer and running a law center but I make sure my life has balance and margin so I can live a life overflowing with purpose and love.

Let Love Remain

Love remains; it does not end with death. What truly matters is for you to be remembered for your love. The love you leave behind will be your legacy. Author Bob Goff inspires us to put our faith into action by doing something simple for someone because we love them. Goff says, "We'll be known for our opinions but remembered for our love."[63] He reminds us the love we leave behind will be our legacy—we won't be missed because of the lectures we gave or arguments we won. Instead, at the end of each of our lives, people will say what they'll miss the most is the small ways we loved the people around us. We will not be defined by our knowledge or what we accomplished, we'll be missed because someone will want to call us to share a joy from the day and remember we're no longer there to share the celebration. These are examples of how the love we leave behind becomes our legacy. He says, "It will be our kindness, not our qualifications, that outlast us."[64] So, leave love behind so you can be remembered for your love. Let your legacy of love remain here on Earth with your loved ones until you are reunited in Heaven to spend eternity together.

Give God Your Heart

Writing love letters concerns matters of the heart, so before you write your final "I love you!" make sure you give God your heart. Goff says,

63 Goff, 59.

64 Goff, 59.

"God's more interested in our hearts than in our plans."[65] Goff's words remind me of Proverbs 23:26, "My son, give me your heart and let your eyes delight in my ways" (NIV). When you love God, and delight in His ways you give Him your heart and your full attention instead of your plans. When your heart belongs to God, you draw close to God by living in pursuit of a deeper faith. He will ignite your heart for legacy so His wondrous works will be remembered. God fills your heart with love so you feel loved and you share your love with others. 1 John 4:7 says, "Dear friends, let us continue to love one another, for love comes from God. Anyone who loves is a child of God and knows God" (NLT). This verse reminds us God loves others through us. As God's children, He created us to be loved by Him and to love Him back so give Him your heart.

The Standard Of Love

Jesus taught us to love God with all our hearts, souls, and minds. Matthew 22:37, Jesus replied, "You must love the Lord your God with all your heart, all your soul, and all your mind" (NLT). This teaching of Jesus is also captured in the book of Mark but adds one more element: strength. Mark 12:30 says, "You must love the Lord your God with all your heart, all your soul, all your mind, and all your strength" (NLT). To love God and to love others with all your strength takes devotion. To completely understand this verse, I want to share Pastor Rick Warren's insight: "You could also say it like this: Love God with all your talk, all your feelings, all your thinking, and all your acting. God shaped you to primarily be a talker, feeler, thinker, or doer."[66] This verse emphasizes the standard of love. It shows us how we should love God—with all our heart, all our soul, all our mind and all our strength. This verse also provides the standard of love for our loved ones, the people God created to care for us, and the people God created us to care for. Writing a legacy love letter is tangible proof you loved with all your heart, all your soul, all your mind, and all your strength. So now you know the standard of love and you can live each day loving God and loving others with all your talk, all your

65 Goff, 277.

66 Warren, Rick. "Stop Talking About It and Start Doing It." *Pastor Rick's Daily Hope*, 28 May 2024, https://pastorrick.com/stop-talking-about-it-and-start-doing-it-2/.

feelings, all your thinking, and all your acting. So express your love to God and others with everything you've got.

All Of Me Loves All Of You

To love with all your heart, all your soul, all your mind, and all your strength would include every part of you. This standard of love reminds me of the song, "All of Me."[67] This popular song is not just for love here on earth. Author Julie Schendel heard John Legend's song and concluded, "When we look at this song through the lens of our relationship with Christ, it can be truly beautiful to sing, 'Give your all to me, I'll give my all to you.' What would it look like if we gave all that we are and all that we had to Jesus? What would it be like to believe a God that tells us that even when we're struggling, even when we're crying, even when the world is beating us down, God is there for us? God is the beginning and the end, the Alpha and Omega. God is our everything."[68] From now on whenever I hear this song or see the slogan, "All of me loves all of you," I will think of Julie's encouragement to give all that we are and all that we have, which is our heart, soul and mind.

Love Is A Choice

The Bible reminds us we can choose to love or not to love because love is a choice. 1 Corinthians 14:1 says, "Go after a life of love as if your life depended on it—because it does" (MSG). If you "go after" something, you make a choice. Love is a choice; you choose to love or not to love. To live a life that brings glory to God, go after a life of love because your life depends on it. Choose each day to love the people God has entrusted you with. When we choose to love every day, we are living a life of true devotion and living a more meaningful life of legacy. The same verse but a different translation emphasizes this lifelong pursuit by showing us we must not only choose to love or not to love but to let love be our highest goal. 1 Corinthians 14:1 directs us, "Let love be your highest

---

67 Legend, John. "All of Me." *Love In The Future.* Written by John Roger Stephens and Toby Gad. Columbia Records, 2013, https://johnlegend.com/.

68 Schendel, Julie. "All of Me Loves All of You." *Julie Schendel,* 17 April 2014, https://julieschendel.wordpress.com/2014/04/17/all-of-me-loves-all-of-you/.

goal" (NLT). When love is our highest goal, we glorify God because we are putting Him above all things as we prioritize showing love in everything we do. By making loving God and loving others our constant focus and our deepest desire, love becomes our highest aspiration. Upon our passing, our legacy of love remains because love was our highest goal. We'll glorify God by leaving behind our love and our legacy will be in the people we loved because we demonstrated the love of God in everything we did.

An Act Of Love

God created you to live a legacy life, to be remembered and to have impact. The Bible says love is something you do, an action. Writing a legacy love letter is something you do, an act of love. When you pour out your heart and soul into a letter, your act of love and your words of love capture the recipient's heart. God's desire for your legacy is for you to love Him and to love others because love is the most important legacy gift. God has shown us how to leave a lasting legacy—fill your life with love.

Let Us Really Love Them

We are called to love others with both our words and actions. 1 John 3:18 directs us, "Dear children, let us not love with words or speech but with actions and in truth" (NIV). Let's ***really*** love our loved ones by taking action by writing a legacy love letter they can hold in their hands and save forever. Even if this task is daunting and you are struggling, start first with love. If you are facing a blank page, you can write, "I love you!" or "I am writing this legacy love letter so you will always remember I love you!" By writing your legacy love letter you are showing them truth in action, you are doing more than merely saying you love them.

Express Love Simply

Expressing love can be simple. It reminds me of when my children were young, they enjoyed choosing their valentines to send to their classmates. In fact, my daughter Kate surprised me when she was in pre-Kindergarten because she wanted to make her own valentines. She designed them herself. She chose pink paper, and she cut a heart shape for each classmate. She then signed her name on every heart. It was a simple act of love. She proudly delivered to each of her classmates the signed heart into the makeshift mailboxes. This simple act expressed her love to her classmates and teachers. Expressing love is the most important thing we can do, it doesn't have to be complicated, it can be a simple act of love. A simple act of love may even be a love song. My client Karen shared with me a love song written and sung to her by her late husband Wyman. She has a photo of the last time he sang to her, just four months before his passing. He passed away peacefully in her loving arms on their 40th wedding anniversary. She says she will love him until the end of her days. She says he lives on in their children and grandchildren. She is committed to being a good steward of his legacy. She shared with me a special legacy love letter book about Wyman: A life well-lived and well-loved which includes Karen's Song. To sing Karen's Song, see **Appendix Sample Letters**.

No More Excuses!

Do not delay your commitment to really love others. When you delay this important task, you put off something until later but in reality it will never get done because you are believing the lie that you still have plenty of time. Commit now by declaring, "No more excuses!" Or look for an excuse "to write" not an excuse "not to write." When you make this declaration and start taking action, your loved ones will know how much you really love them. Instead of just saying you love them, your action of writing a letter says "I love you!" which will always remind them you really loved them. Your loved ones will feel really loved by you and really loved by God. Bob Goff says no one is remembered for what they just planned to do. Goff writes, "Just like great characters in films are remembered by what they *do* and not by what they merely think about, we're known for our actions. The power of love is in the sacrifice and commitment it requires. Sacrifice and commitment always travel with love and action. Love looks like showing up with hands to help even when we don't know what to do. Love looks like stopping by even if we don't know what to say. Simply put, love doesn't just think about it; love does it."[69] So apply this reasoning to your legacy love letters and if you

69 Goff, 13.

start to delay this important task say out loud, "Love does it!" When you follow through on the plan to demonstrate your love with a completed letter, it demonstrates your love in real life and you will be remembered for what you did in love, not what you merely thought about.

Don't Get Stuck!

You may feel stuck which might interfere with your commitment to leave a legacy of love. Don't get bogged down with questions about the rules and etiquette for writing the messages you want to leave. You may experience writer's block because you are feeling pressure that the letter must be perfect since this will be your final goodbye. Just remember the goal is a completed legacy love letter; it doesn't need to be perfect. Writer's block may come in the form of procrastination. You may be procrastinating because you think you still have plenty of time to complete your letters. You may be paralyzed with fear because you don't know how to begin. Don't get stuck on choosing the right paper and the right ink. I am not an expert in the art of letter press but I love paper goods and sealing stickers, so I chose to elevate my legacy love letters by choosing nice cards and stationery. My friend Anne would tell you not to worry about it, her mother's letter was written on binder paper and it still became a sacred part of her grieving process because her mother's voice, love, and presence were captured in ink.

Love Letters For All Occasions

You can break through writer's block by practicing writing love letters. You can write love letters for any given occasion. Even if you didn't intend the card to be your legacy love letter, your heartfelt note card may be the last love letter your loved one receives from you before you die, or they die. The last love letter I wrote my dad was the Father's Day card he received just before he died. I didn't know it would be his last, but I wanted him to know how much I loved him. My client Carol cherishes the last birthday card she received from her sister. She has it framed where she can see it when she wakes up in the morning. Your note card may be cherished for years to come. Some people choose to leave cards to be opened at a later occasion or milestone birthday. My husband's aunt

Sheryl left a 40th Birthday card for him sixteen years before he turned 40 just in case she wasn't alive to deliver the card herself. She was still living and was able to deliver the card herself but it still had the original date of August 1, 1996. The note on the envelope read: "***In case I'm no longer living on Erik's 40th birthday, please give this card to him. Love, Sheryl***" She also typed a legacy letter inside the card. "***I hope I'm alive to wish you a happy 40th birthday, but if I'm not, I just wanted you to know … how much joy you gave me when you were young, how much pride I've had in you as a young adult, and how much love I will always carry in my heart for you.***" To read her note and letter see **Appendix Sample Letters**.

Train Up A Child

One of the most quoted verses about parenting is found in Proverbs 22:6, "Train up a child in the way he should go; even when he is old he will not depart from it" (ESV). Solomon wrote and compiled most of the book of Proverbs. It teaches people how to attain wisdom, discipline, and a prudent life, and how to do what is right, just and fair. It is an excellent guide to how to live a godly life. Our job as parents is to live a godly life and to help our children learn the skills they need to do what is right, just and fair. It begins with us as parents modeling a willingness to use our gifts to serve and to love God and to love others in words and action. Our legacy letters train them in the way they should go as they learn how to love God and to love others in words and action. I learned this lesson firsthand when my daughter Kate graduated from high school. I chose a graduation letter book which had ten envelopes with writing prompts and two blank envelopes. The book included prompts to write letters to the graduate. I challenged myself to answer each prompt but I also reached out to family members the week of graduation to help me with this special gift. Nobody responded to my email or asked me about it but on the morning of graduation it was my son who was the first person to give me a letter to be added to the book. I was so proud of him and pleased with his efforts to love his sister well on the day of her high school graduation. She took the letter book with her when she moved away for college. Her older brother's words had an impact on her life as a college freshman because he had written words of love and encouragement by sharing with her helpful advice including, "***I wish someone had given me this good advice: college isn't harder than high school, it's just a lot more work.***" He promised her he would be there for her if there was anything she needed. He also reminded her, "***You'll do great in college.***" When we speak truth in love, our children will speak truth in love and our legacy of love remains.

Trust in God's Love

Earlier in this chapter we read 1 John 4:16, "God is love" (CEV) because this verse declares the truth about God and the truth about love. Studying another translation of this verse, we discover not only is God love but we live in love when we live in God and put our trust in His love. 1 John 4:16 says, "We know how much God loves us, and we have put our trust in his love. God is love, and all who live in love live in God, and God lives in them" (NLT). He gives us the power to love. His love quiets our fears and gives us confidence. To live a legacy life in pursuit of a deeper faith and a more meaningful life, we must put our trust in God's love.

Love Each Other

God is love and God loves us perfectly. He will love us through others and love others through us. He commands us to love each other in John 13:34, "So now I am giving you a new commandment: Love each other. Just as I have loved you, you should love each other" (NLT). I also chose this scripture to represent part two of this book because loving God and loving others is the legacy that matters. The Message translation of this verse teaches us why we are commanded to love each other. When we love each other, everyone will recognize that we are His disciples. John 13:34-35 commands, "Let me give you a new command: Love one another. In the same way I loved you, you love one another. This is how everyone will recognize that you are my disciples—when they see the love you have for each other" (MSG). Your loved ones see love in your legacy letter which will be read whenever there is doubt. Love reveals itself in our actions as we demonstrate God's love and love each other.

A Love Letter Farewell

One of my clients wrote a love letter farewell to her husband who died of complications following a surgery. During his final days a hospital bed was set up in the family room and soft music was playing in the background. She went into the den and wrote her letter. She thought of the poem by Elizabeth Barrett Browning, "How Do I Love Thee? (Sonnet 43)"[70] and she listed all the things she loved about her husband. Later that afternoon she told him she had something to read to him, and he died that night. Her story is simply beautiful because she was prompted to write the letter and share the letter. The poem was her inspiration in writing the love letter. Knowing her husband was going to pass soon, she realized it was time to share the letter with him. As she shared her precious story with me, I felt like I was in the room with them witnessing the beautiful legacy gift. The heartfelt gift was for both of them, the giver and the receiver. The special moment they shared was a gift from God just before He took her husband home to Heaven. You can read this poem and her letter, see **Appendix Sample Letters**.

Scripture Prompt: "Study More!"

> "Dear children, let us not love with words or speech but with actions and in truth."—1 John 3:18 (NIV)

Prayer Prompt: "Pray Now!"

Dear Lord,

We praise you for loving each one of us with your everlasting love. Help us live lives overflowing with purpose and love. We pray our final words will have staying power and our loved ones never forget how much we love them. Let us stop just saying we love people; let us really love them, and show it by our actions.

Amen

---

70 Browning, Elizabeth Barrett. "How Do I Love Thee? (Sonnet 43)." *Poets.org*, Academy of American Poets, 1850, https://poets.org/poem/how-do-i-love-thee-sonnet-43. Accessed 14 Aug. 2025.

Writing Prompt: "Write Now!"

Journal and reflect about why you want to express love to your loved ones before it is too late. Write about something that inspires you to express your love just like the poem chosen by the woman in the story about the love letter farewell.

Worship Prompt: "Listen Now!"

"Love God Love People" by Danny Gokey[71]

This song by Danny Gokey reminds us not only is love patient and kind, but it also rescues hearts and changes lives. This worship song embodies the commandment to love God and love others as we love God and love people. When we sing along about love being patient and kind, we are reminded of 1 Corinthians 13:4-7. We are reminded the love of God rescues hearts and changes lives. We get so busy with our to-do lists and checking all the boxes so we all need a reminder of what we are striving for. The song reminds us to simplify our pursuits because it all comes down to this: all we have to do is love God and love people. We are reminded that loving God is deeply connected to loving and helping others. This song is a perfect reminder for our legacy love letters, too. When we realize it all comes down to loving God and loving people then we can simplify our worldly pursuits and focus instead on living a life in pursuit of a deeper faith and a more meaningful life. Our life has meaning when we love and help our loved ones. When we love God and love people our legacy of love remains, it does not end with death.

---

71 Danny Gokey. "Love God Love People (feat. Michael W. Smith)." *Haven't Seen It Yet.* Written by Danny Gokey, Colby Wedgeworth, Ben Glover, Riley Clemmons, and Jeff Sojka. Sparrow Records, under exclusive license to Capitol CMG, Inc., 2019. https://www.dannygokey.com/.

Chapter Ten

T -Trust God: Express Faith

Your legacy gift will glorify God when you speak Truth in love with faith and confidence. God's plans for your life and His purpose for your legacy is to express love and demonstrate His love in words and actions as you T—Trust Him and express your faith. This chapter emphasizes how to leave a legacy gift of faith for your loved ones. Your legacy love letter is a letter of faith and eternal hope when your final words remind your loved ones your goodbye is only temporary since you will be reunited with them again in Heaven one day. When you share your faith with your loved ones, your legacy of faith is passed on as an inheritance, handed down from one generation to the next.

Your Legacy Gift Of Faith

In the case of legacy love letters, the special ingredient you need to complete this writing project will come from your Heavenly Father who loves you and has created a legacy for you of love, faith, hope, and gratitude. The special ingredient you will need to make a difference with the legacy love letters you will deliver will be your faith. God's heart for your legacy is more than fighting the good fight and finishing your race. When God brings you home you will say, "I have kept the faith" (2 Timothy 4:7, NIV). As you deliver your legacy gift of faith, your loved ones will see by your words and actions you were faithful to the very end because of God's great love. Our faith is a gift from God to be shared with our loved ones so they too can be saved. Ephesians 2:8 says, "For it is by grace you have been saved, through faith—and this is not from yourselves, it is the gift of God—" (NIV).

Trust God's Truthfulness

God is holy, trustworthy and unchangeable. We can trust God and rely on the Bible because God is truthful; He does not lie. He is trustworthy because He does not leave His promises unfulfilled. This biblical truth is found in Numbers 23:19, "God is not like people, who lie; He is not a human who changes his mind. Whatever he promises, he does; He speaks, and it is done" (GNT).

Colossians 3:16 says, "Let the message about Christ, in all its richness, fill your lives. Teach and counsel each other with all the wisdom he gives. Sing psalms and hymns and spiritual songs to God with thankful hearts" (NLT). This verse reminds us how to fill our lives with truth as we fill our lives with the message about Christ. We are to share the message about Christ with our loved ones by teaching and counseling them with all the wisdom He has given us.

Trust God's Faithfulness

God is trustworthy because He is faithful and He does not leave His promises unfulfilled. Trust Him because He loves you. Dedicate your life to Him because He is faithful. Deuteronomy 7:9 reminds us, "Know therefore that the Lord your God is God; he is the faithful God, keeping his covenant of love to a thousand generations of those who love him and keep his commandments" (NIV). When you know that "God is God," you will have the faith that you need and you can trust God's faithfulness.

You can remind your loved ones to trust God's faithfulness and you can write, "***Know therefore that the Lord your God is God; he is the faithful God, keeping his covenant of love to a thousand generations of those who love him and keep his commandments.***"

In Pursuit Of A Deeper Faith

Hebrews 11:6 reminds us, "And without faith it is impossible to please God, because anyone who comes to him must believe that he exists and that he rewards those who earnestly seek him" (NIV). This verse reminds us to have faith and believe God exists or it will be impossible to please God. This verse promises us God rewards those who earnestly seek Him. When we earnestly seek Him, we are living in pursuit of a deeper faith.

Faith Expresses Itself Through Love

The most important thing in a Christian life is demonstrating one's faith through actions of love towards others. Galatians 5:6 says, "The only thing that counts is faith expressing itself through love" (NIV). In this essential verse for Christian living, the apostle Paul argues true faith is shown through love. Your legacy love letter has an everlasting impact since your faith is expressing itself through love.

Remembering God's Works

Legacy is remembering God's works. Your final words have an impact for God. Tell your children and grandchildren about the miracles God did. Teach your loved ones what you've seen and heard and what God has done for you. When we remember God's works, they will not fade from our hearts. Deuteronomy 4:9 tells us, "But be very careful! Never forget the things that you yourselves have seen. Remember these things for as long as you live. Tell your children and your grandchildren about all the things that God has done" (EASY). When we tell our loved ones what God has done for us, they can see the times in our lives when God expressed kindness. Sharing our hope stories encourages others because God has the power to transform their lives and will provide a way for them to move from being stuck to freedom if they choose to accept His mercy and grace. When we see and hear of what God has done, we have hope and follow Him. We rededicate our lives to Him by loving Him completely and obeying His commands because of who He is and what He has done for us. God's heart for legacy is revealed in all the things He has done to fulfill His purpose so remember God's works.

Scripture Prompt: "Study More!"

> "The only thing that counts is faith expressing itself through love." —Galatians 5:6 (NIV).

Prayer Prompt: "Pray Now!"

Dear Lord,

We thank you for your truth and faithfulness. Help us express our faith through love so we can leave a legacy gift that glorifies you. Help us teach our loved ones what we've seen and heard and what you've done for us so they can remember your good works.

Amen

Writing Prompt: "Write Now!"

Take time to reflect and journal about the miracles God has done in your life. Legacy is remembering God's works. What do you want your loved ones to remember about what you've seen and heard and what God has done for you? Think about the times you've seen God working in your loved ones' lives, too. Do you need to remind your loved ones about what you've seen and heard and what God has done for them? What will your last words to those you love be?

Worship Prompt: "Listen Now!"

"I Belong To Jesus" by Paul and Hannah McClure[72]

This song reminds us since we belong to Jesus we are never alone, and we are never abandoned. This worship song helps us recognize Jesus as our shepherd, our keeper, our provider, and our protector. We sing the words of Psalm 23:4 when we sing, "Yea, though I walk through the valley of the shadow of death, I will fear no evil" (NKJV). These words are familiar to us because these words bring us comfort and help us surrender our fear of death. To fully understand Psalm 23, I recommend the book *Traveling Light* by pastor and author Max Lucado.[73] His book teaches about the promise of Psalm 23 and how we can release the burdens we were never intended to bear. In this helpful book, the author identifies the burdens of a lesser god; self-reliance; discontent; weariness; worry; hopelessness; guilt; arrogance; the grave; grief, fear, loneliness, shame, disappointment, envy, doubt, and homesickness. The author explains why David was able to claim, "I will fear no evil" because he knew where to look. This explanation illustrates how we should live like David because David went first to his Father unlike the rest of us who go to the bar, the counselor, the self-help book or the friend next door.[74]

72 The McClures. "I Belong To Jesus (Studio Version)." *Homecoming*. Written by Paul McClure, Hannah McClure, and Sean Curran. Bethel Music, 2021, https://paulandhannahmcclure.com/.

73 Lucado, Max. *Traveling Light: Releasing the Burdens You Were Never Intended to Bear*. Nashville, TN, Thomas Nelson, 2001, vii-viii.

74 Lucado, 127.

Chapter Eleven

R – Really Love Them: Express Forgiveness

Your legacy gift brings glory to God when you speak Truth in love with faith and confidence. God's plans for your life and His purpose for your legacy is to express love and demonstrate His love in words and actions as you *R–Really Love Them: Express Forgiveness.* To love fully, is to really love them and express love with forgiveness because love keeps no record of wrongs. 1 Corinthians 13:5, says, Love "keeps no record of wrongs" (NIV). Author Gary Chapman says, "Forgiveness is an expression of love."[75] The goal of legacy writing is to ensure you have not left anything unsaid. You may need to include a sincere apology or a request for forgiveness in your legacy love letter so

75 Chapman, Gary. *The Five Love Languages: How To Express Heartfelt Commitment To Your Mate.* Chicago, IL, Northfield Publishing, 1992, 1995, 2004, 47-48.

you can really love them by expressing forgiveness. This may be difficult on your own so you will need to rely on Jesus to heal your brokenness and your broken relationships.

Don't Just Pretend To Love Others

Romans 12:9 reminds us, "Don't just pretend to love others. Really love them. Hate what is wrong. Hold tightly to what is good" (NLT). This scripture reminds us love must be sincere so we must take action if we want to love others well. We've got to stop pretending to love others and really love them by our behaviors and actions. Sincere love requires concentration and effort so we can love one another deeply from the heart. Do not lose heart! Legacy letter writing is a challenging task but not impossible. The rewards for a completed letter are priceless so you must do the work and overcome any obstacles.

Be Kind And Compassionate

Ephesians 4:32 says, "Be kind and compassionate to one another, forgiving each other, just as in Christ God forgave you" (NIV). This verse reminds us to be kind and compassionate. When we are kind and compassionate to others, we can walk in the obedience of forgiveness by choosing to love them instead of resenting them. God doesn't want us to carry grudges, resentment or bitterness. We are called to release unforgiveness quickly so it doesn't interfere with our relationship with God and our relationships with others. When we learn the obedience of forgiveness, we are demonstrating our love to God and others.

Forgive Them

We are called to forgive our loved ones so our Heavenly Father can forgive us. Mark 11:25 directs us, "And when you stand praying, if you hold anything against anyone, forgive them, so that your Father in heaven may forgive you your sins" (NIV). God does not keep a list of wrongdoings, so we are not to keep a list either. When we forgive, we maintain strong and fulfilling relationships which are key to living a more meaningful life. When we let go of hurts and abandon grudges, we can forgive others, which leads to harmony and forgiveness. God's forgiveness is complete. Christians are saved by faith, not by good deeds. When we love God and others it's because we have been forgiven. Jesus said those who are forgiven much love much. Luke 7:47 says, "So I tell you, this woman has done many bad things. But I have forgiven her. She loves me a lot, because I have forgiven her for many bad things. If I only forgive someone a little, that person only loves me a little" (EASY). This verse assures us Jesus has rescued His followers from eternal death. It reminds us we must forgive much. To leave a legacy gift of forgiveness glorifies God.

Express Love With An Apology

Nobody is perfect, we have all done or said things we wish we could take back. An apology is an opportunity to acknowledge your mistake. You don't have to make it complicated, simply write: "***I'm sorry***." This is your opportunity to acknowledge your mistakes before you die. Search your heart—is there a regret you are holding onto? When I look back and think about the things I wish I could do differently, I think of the times I was late picking up kids from school or activities or just getting home for dinner on time. I want to make an apology to my husband and my children for the times in my life my failure to manage my time left them feeling like my clients or my work were more important than them. I have learned how to set better boundaries this past year when I had to protect my time to write this book. Writing my first published book has been a dream come true. The most challenging part has been protecting my time to make sure I set aside time to write. To stay on track with book deadlines I had to say "no" to opportunities, both professional or personal, which were not right for me in this season. The skill of learning to say "no" to things that do not align with a priority empowered me to protect my time, energy, and resources. To protect my writing time, I also reduced my caseload and obligations at the office. I set my alarm to write before my work day started. The sacrifices were definitely worth it, but I regret not having these skills when my children were young so they didn't have to wait for me when I was running late because my office commitments interfered with my home obligations.

Express Love With A Request For Forgiveness

To really love our loved ones, we can express love with a request for forgiveness. Depending on the circumstances, you may need to communicate more than an apology with the following statements:

> ***"There's no excuse for how I treated you."***
>
> ***"You have every right to feel the way you do."***
>
> ***"It was wrong of me to … "***

If this chapter on forgiveness is for you, you will want to spend some additional time in prayer and reflection. Be willing to examine yourself, including your attitudes, thoughts, motives, words, or actions. You can pray as David did in Psalm 139: 23-24, "Search me, God, and know my heart; test me and know my anxious thoughts. See if there is any offensive way in me, and lead me in the way everlasting" (NIV). Depending on the circumstances, you may need to talk to a counselor about your specific situation. For additional understanding and encouragement, I recommend reading *Forgiveness: Overcoming the Impossible* by Mathew West.[76] He shares powerful stories of people who faced some of life's hardest moments including betrayal, abandonment, divorce, addiction and death. Each of the stories Mathew shares in his book demonstrate how they allowed God to do the impossible and work through them and offer forgiveness. He shows his readers how to take the steps to be set free so they can break the chains of unforgiveness and guilt.

Estrangement Needs Forgiveness

Even though our relationships are essential to life, they are not always easy. Your legacy love letter may need to reconcile a broken or estranged relationship. If you are in a broken or estranged relationship, you will need to forgive someone or ask someone for forgiveness.

As an estate planning attorney, I have worked with clients over the years who have chosen to disinherit a loved one as a result of a broken or estranged relationship. The act of disinheriting a family member is

76 West, Matthew. *Forgiveness: Overcoming The Impossible.* Nashville, TN, Thomas Nelson, 2013.

a difficult and heavy decision for anyone to make no matter what the circumstances. I take time to discuss their reasons and the backstory. As their attorney, it is not my place to judge them or their loved one or decide if they've made the right choice. I do take notes so I can be ready to testify in court if the person who is disinherited later contests or disagrees with their exclusion. The client's explanation or reasons for the disinheritance of a family member are not contained in the will or trust. I advise them regarding their documents and I explain the wording that is used, "***I intentionally omit to provide for …***"

In California, a legal heir who has standing to contest a document is a spouse or a biological child who has been ***intentionally omitted***. In one case, a woman disinherited her soon-to-be ex-husband. When she died before her divorce was final, her surviving spouse contested her document, which means he tried to cancel it. If he had been successful in canceling her document, then her Last Will and Testament would have been thrown out of court and he would have been considered an heir of her estate. She had the legal right to disinherit him, but he contested the validity of the document because he did not want to be disinherited despite their pending divorce.

As a Christian, I am called to be a peacemaker. Even though not all my clients are believers, I can still encourage them by reminding them that if circumstances change and they are able to reconcile the relationship, they are welcome to come back to my office at a later date to remove the disinheritance provision and rewrite the distribution plan.

Unfortunately, in some circumstances, the prospect of removing the disinheritance provision later is not always an option. In some cases, it is because the disinherited individual is struggling with drug or alcohol addiction and the receipt of an inheritance would cause danger to them. In one case, while my client was in a care facility, her son removed all of her possessions from her residence. When she returned home to live out her final days, her son refused to return her belongings. He had not just removed a few select items, he had removed everything from her home. She did have the legal standing to sue him for elder abuse, but she chose not to. Instead, she chose to terminate her relationship with him and disinherit him from her estate. After meeting with her several times to discuss the circumstances and the proposed disinheritance clause, I chose to arrange a recorded deposition just in case her son decided to object to his disinheritance and legally contest her decision. She has since passed and there was no contest once her son's counsel was informed of the elder abuse action she had against her son which she chose not to pursue. It was definitely an unfortunate case, but her proactive steps in disinheriting him were necessary based on the circumstances. Drastic measures were taken because her son was no longer a rightful beneficiary of her estate. Her son abused her by stealing her possessions and not returning them despite her many requests. He chose her possessions over a continued relationship with her. If she were alive today, I would share a copy of this book with her and encourage her to write a legacy love letter with forgiveness.

Bad Decisions Need Grace

When facing guilt and shame from broken relationships, do not lose heart; be encouraged God uses human error and sin for His good purposes. Whenever you are overwhelmed by a bad decision you or someone else has made, be comforted knowing God will use it for His good purposes. This happened to Joseph in the Old Testament after his brothers sold him into slavery. Instead of responding in bitterness, Joseph responded with grace and said, "You intended to harm me, but God intended it for good to accomplish what is now being done, the saving of many lives" (Genesis 50:20, NIV). This Bible story is encouraging because Joseph faced ultimate betrayal by his own family members and yet that was not the end of the story. This is an example of how God had a bigger and better plan for Joseph's life. This verse also teaches us how to respond with grace instead of responding in bitterness when someone has harmed us with a bad decision.

To reflect further on how Joseph reacted to his brothers, consider The Message translation. Genesis 50:19-21 shows us the contemporary English version of this passage, "Joseph replied, 'Don't be afraid. Do I act for God? Don't you see, you planned evil against me but God used those same plans for my good, as you see all around you right now—life for many people. Easy now, you have nothing to fear; I'll take care of you and your children.' He reassured them, speaking with them heart-to-heart" (MSG). We know from Joseph's story when others plan evil against us God can use those same plans for our good.

Focus On Reconciliation

Pastor and author Rick Warren has identified the keys to a blessed life which includes how to reconcile a relationship. In teaching how to reconcile a relationship, he identifies seven steps to resolving conflict. He advises, "The only way to resolve a conflict is to face it."[77] Unfortunately, with most conflicts, you will need to focus on reconciliation, not resolution. Pastor Rick reminds us resolution can only be achieved by the parties by resolving ***every*** disagreement. This is an impossible goal. As an estate attorney, I have represented many parties in direct conflict, and I can verify there is no way ***every*** disagreement can be resolved. Before a court trial can be set, the court orders the parties to a mandatory settlement conference. In California, there is no way to avoid this requirement. Parties must earn their court date which means they must prove they tried to settle their dispute, but they were unable to, so they still require the assistance of the court to make a final ruling or a judgment.

To be successful in reaching a settlement for an estate dispute, parties must agree to disagree so they can compromise and agree to divide what's left. The settlement is successful when all parties feel like they had to compromise or give up on what they believed they were entitled to. I have never met anybody who was happy about a compromise. However, they can agree they needed to end the dispute to salvage not only what was left of the estate but to protect their own health and well-being. The parties then focus on reconciliation, not resolution.

Forgiveness Brings Peace

Pastor Rick reminds us to focus on reconciliation which means to reestablish the relationship. Reconciliation for some may not happen during their lifetime. A legacy love letter can be written to reconcile a relationship upon your passing to make peace with your loved one. Matthew 5:9 says, "Blessed are the peacemakers, for they will be called children of God" (NIV). Peacemaking is recommended to resolve conflict and restore broken relationships. Dedicate time for prayer and reflection and ask God to show you if there is a conflict you have been avoiding

77 Warren, Rick. *The Keys To A Blessed Life Study Guide.* Rancho Santa Margarita, CA, Purpose Driven Communications, 2015, 36.

or denying. Search your heart and identify a broken relationship which needs mending. Pastor Rick teaches practical steps you can take to resolve conflict and restore a broken relationship. He says conflicts are caused by selfish desires, pride, and our inability to listen before speaking. Ask God for wisdom so you will know what God wants you to do in taking steps to reconcile the broken relationship which leads to forgiveness and peace.[78]

Your Hard Story is a Hope Story

God sees your heavy heart and your grief over this broken or estranged relationship. This is a chapter in your story you probably do not want to read out loud. But God has a better plan for you and your legacy story. I know this for a fact because I have been encouraged by my author community at hope*books. Each hope*author is a testament of God using each hard story for a hope story. God chose me to write the book about legacy love letters because of my expertise in the field of estate planning. But friends, God also chose me to write the book about legacy love letters so He could draw me closer to Him during my season of grief following loss. God wanted me to look toward Him for strength and comfort.

Despite my season of grief, God had a better legacy story for me when my business strategy coach Anne Watson recommended I attend the January 2024 hope*story conference in Sarasota, Florida. The marketing materials promised the conference would be a transformative event designed to help me discover, share, and publish my unique story of hope. The conference had a huge impact on me. Even before the conference ended, I sent my coach an email because I wanted to share with her I had accepted my calling as an author by signing up with hope*books. I wanted her to know immediately I was now committed to sharing my words in a book. I thought I was there to hire, or at least interview, a hybrid publishing company who was promising my book in my hands in 12 months. Instead, I found a team of professionals who were volunteering for the position of supporting me. They were encouraging me to take 100% responsibility for my book journey. They already knew

78 Warren, 35-36.

I had a message to share and an audience to serve. They knew I wanted to be faithful, not famous, as I shared my how-to secrets of writing legacy love letters. They knew God had entrusted me with a bold message which they would not water down because my "See you in Heaven" message was countercultural. I was convinced the world needed my hope-filled words more now than ever before as I embarked on the journey to share my work with Christians who wanted to leave a legacy of love, faith, hope and gratitude for their loved ones who will need comfort, healing, and closure upon their passing. Their heartfelt final goodbye will be found and read and cherished by loved ones who will not be left empty-handed and will grieve differently because they will hold onto the hope of heaven as they will look forward to the day they will be reunited in heaven with loved ones.

The theme for the conference was written on the tote bag and the T-shirt, "Mining Your Past for Diamonds from Rejection to Redemption." On the flight home I was spending time reflecting and reviewing my notes. I realized I had been in denial about my hard story. I knew God had called me to write a book about legacy love letters and I knew I was there to choose my publisher. I immediately texted a new friend from the conference who had impacted me by sharing her hard story. I thanked her for sharing her hard story and I needed to share that I had been in denial all week pretending the theme did not apply to me. I shared with her that God had revealed to me that "past" didn't just mean hurts growing up. I was still in the middle of the mess because my hard story was still occurring: I was experiencing the loss of my identical twin sister from estrangement and the loss of my dad who had died suddenly following a stroke. It had been a hard year of loss and grief, yet I knew God was going to use my hard story so I could help and encourage others with my hope*story. I am confident our hard stories of struggles and difficult circumstances are not wasted. My confidence comes from the biblical promise in Romans 8:28 that God causes everything to work together for the good of those who love Him. As believers in Christ, we have confidence our pain and suffering refine and strengthen our faith, making us useful to God. We can respond to difficult trials with confidence, since God knows, plans, and directs our lives for the good as He leads us to a better future.

Scripture Prompt: "Study More!"

> "Be kind and compassionate to one another, forgiving each other, just as in Christ God forgave you." —Ephesians 4:32 (NIV)

Prayer Prompt: "Pray Now!"

Dear Lord,

We praise you today for being our source of forgiveness. Thank you for your ultimate sacrifice of your son. Help us be kind and compassionate and forgive our loved ones as you have forgiven us. Since we are called to love others and forgiveness is an expression of love.

Amen

Writing Prompt: "Write Now!"

Journal and reflect about God's forgiveness during your lifetime. Have you experienced broken and estranged relationships? Reflect on times God loved you even when you were being unlovable. Write about where you are feeling God is asking you to forgive others. Consider focusing on reconciliation, not resolution of every disagreement. This approach will help you express love with forgiveness.

Worship Prompt: "Listen Now!"

"Forgiveness" by Matthew West[79]

The key verse is Ephesians 4:32, "Be kind and compassionate to one another, forgiving each other, just as in Christ God forgave you" (NIV). This song reminds us forgiveness allows us to do the impossible which is to love the unlovable. When we forgive, we are set free. When we forgive, we love the unlovable. Matthew West made it his mission to discover

79 West, Matthew. "Forgiveness." *Into the Light.* Sparrow Records, 2012, https://www.matthewwest.com/.

the power of the stories of forgiveness. Each of the stories he selected for his book revealed the difference between pain and joy, brokenness and healing, confinement and freedom.[80] He encourages his readers to ask our Savior which choice is right for us and He will guide us and empower us to walk the path that leads to restoration, reconciliation, and peace with others.[81]

80 West, *Forgiveness: Overcoming the Impossible*, xvi-xvii.

81 West, *Forgiveness: Overcoming the Impossible*, 76.

Chapter Twelve

U – Unstoppable: Express Encouragement

You will leave a legacy gift that glorifies God when you express encouragement to your loved ones. 1 Corinthians 13:7 says, "Love never gives up, never loses faith, is always hopeful, and endures through every circumstance" (NLT). God's plans for your life and His purpose for your legacy is to express love and demonstrate His love in words and actions as you express encouragement and help your loved ones become Unstoppable because love never gives up, never loses faith, is always hopeful, and endures through every circumstance.

Unstoppable Love Never Gives Up

When we offer genuine support to our loved ones, our love protects them and helps them persevere. We share our encouraging words so our loved ones can become unstoppable. When facing loss and grief, our loved ones need encouragement because the shock of death is debilitating and paralyzing. We need to remind them to get up again just like a fighter who has been knocked out or a skier who has fallen. Sometimes we must lead them back to the path they were on before they received the devastating news. Other times we have to remind them to put one foot in front of the other just like a long-distance runner on the last mile. Our encouragement reminds them love never gives up and they feel loved despite their loss and grief. With our love and encouragement, our loved ones can finish the race God designed specifically for them despite their loss and grief.

Love Encourages Like A Coach

When fulfilling your role as a legacy writer you can borrow from coaching. A coach is a person dedicated to building character and maximizing potential. A coach also teaches, supports, and mentors. Growing up, I had a wonderful ice-skating coach named Evelynne. She taught me how to skate, but she was also dedicated to building my character and maximizing my potential with her words of encouragement. Because she believed in me and what I could accomplish, I was unstoppable and I did not give up. I know I got through middle school and high school because of her coaching me on and off the ice. Because of her desire to see me maximize my potential, she gave me the opportunity to go to Victoria, Canada to live and ice-skate for an entire high school summer. It was her encouragement and belief in me which pushed me to do my very best. She helped open doors for me to find the right place to live and train. To this day, I treasure my memories from my summer in Canada. Even though I never made it to the Olympic winter games, I got to be fully immersed in a sport I loved. This once-in-a-lifetime opportunity built my character as I traveled out of the country, lived away from home, and dedicated my time to be fully committed to the life of an athlete. I had to sacrifice a lazy high school summer of being with friends and living in my own comfort zone. What I gained in return was priceless. I learned how to be fully committed to a dream and how to live outside my comfort zone. My life was blessed by the love of a coach who wanted me to dream big and maximize my potential. I am forever grateful to God for giving me this wonderful coach who poured her love into my life. I don't know for sure because my coach never talked to me about her faith in God, but I believe there is a strong possibility I will see her again in Heaven. Your final words of encouragement are life-giving words which leave an everlasting legacy as they build character in your loved ones and help them maximize their potential. You too can encourage your loved ones like a coach. Anne's mother wrote, "***No matter what you do – do it the best you can.***" Kathleen's dad wrote, "***Do your best always and try to be outstanding in everything you do.***" See **Appendix Sample Letters**.

Unstoppable Love Never Loses Faith

The command to "encourage others" is found throughout the Bible. When you encourage loved ones, you are living for what matters and allowing God to use you to do His work. In 1 Thessalonians 5:11-23, Paul gives many specific examples of how to encourage others: appreciate a quality, rejoice always, pray continually, and give thanks in all circumstances. 1 Thessalonians 5:16-18 commands, "Rejoice always, pray continually, give thanks in all circumstances; for this is God's will for you in Christ Jesus" (NIV). Unstoppable love never loses faith. Obeying these three commands helps us live fully in pursuit of a deeper faith and a more meaningful life as we encourage one another and build each other up.

Unstoppable Love Builds Each Other Up

One way to "build each other up" is to tell loved ones about a quality you appreciate in him or her. 1 Thessalonians 5:11 says "Therefore encourage one another and build each other up, just as in fact you are doing" (NIV). When my youngest daughter graduated from high school, I was blessed by a former law school classmate who encouraged me by telling my daughter about qualities she appreciated in me. In the congratulations card, she told my daughter that her mother was "kind, brilliant and determined." My daughter shared these encouraging words with me and this letter of congratulations not only encouraged my daughter on her high school graduation day, but God used her words to highlight for me the qualities God created in me. These life-giving words meant a lot coming from a law school classmate whom I hadn't seen in years. Even after all this time, she still remembered me and still thought of me as kind, brilliant and determined. God used this card to speak truth into my life as well as my daughter's life. The impact of these life-giving words was felt because this classmate never said them to me before. Until my daughter shared the card, I had no idea my classmate remembered me this way. This card was so encouraging to both my daughter and me. My daughter was impressed by the words and shared the card with me. I was impressed by the words and shared them with my author community and now my readers. This is a real-life example of how our encouraging words have a ripple effect. We never know how God will use our kind words or even the impact of our kind words to encourage others. God's purpose is to make each one of us more like Jesus. God produces these qualities in you and your loved ones. You can remind them of how God is making them more like Jesus by writing, "I see these qualities in you …" When you mention the qualities you see or the qualities you appreciate in your loved ones, you are highlighting the qualities God created in them.

Unstoppable Love Is Always Hopeful

1 Thessalonians 5:16 says, "Rejoice always" (NIV). When we rejoice, we express our joy with cheerful and hopeful hearts. As God fills the pages of our legacy story, we express our hope and joy as we celebrate with our loved ones as they reach important milestones. They feel loved and encouraged when we take time to express our pride in their important achievements. We rejoice and celebrate their graduations from preschool, Kindergarten, primary school, junior high school, high school, college and graduate school. We express our hope and joy when they have passed a driver's test and received their first driver's license. We rejoice and celebrate when they land their first job and again when they secure their dream job. We celebrate the purchase of their first home. You can continue to encourage your loved ones by recalling memories of these important milestones and accomplishments in their life. They will rejoice always because unstoppable love is always hopeful.

Unstoppable Love Prays Continually

1 Thessalonians 5:17 says, "pray continually" (NIV). Encouragement comes from being at peace with God and having a relationship with Him.

God is always with you, so talk to Him. Your legacy letter can encourage and remind your loved ones to "pray continually." When your loved ones remember God is always with them and they are not alone, they will be encouraged and comforted by His presence. As parents we pray for wisdom for our children regarding their work, career, occupation and profession. When we are gone, our prayers for our children will still be answered here on earth. But our prayers cannot be answered if we don't pray continually. As we pray continually, we will trust and obey the plans God has for our loved ones. You can even write out your prayers for your loved ones in your legacy letters. You can write, "I am praying for you …"

Unstoppable Love Gives Thanks

1 Thessalonians 5:18 says, "give thanks in all circumstances; for this is God's will for you in Christ Jesus" (NIV). This verse reminds us that unstoppable love gives thanks. To encourage your loved ones, make a list of all the gifts God has given you, and give thanks to God for each one. Once your gratitude list is completed, review it and then share with your loved one's special memories of time together. You can thank them for a special memory and tell them what you are thankful for. You can write, "My life would not have been the same …" If writing a letter to a parent, spouse, or sibling you may use these encouraging words, "I can't imagine my life without you."

I can't imagine my life without the love and encouragement I received from my spouse. We got married just before I started law school. I am thankful for his love and encouragement through law school, the bar exam, and my law practice. I didn't want to merely write, "Thank you for staying married to me during law school." Instead, I wanted to express gratitude for his encouragement by writing: "***I am thankful you were there to give me support and encouragement in my life; because of you I was able to get through the most challenging time. You were dedicated and committed to making sure I could learn and succeed. Because you did not give up on me or my dream, I was able to persevere. I want to thank you again for supporting me.***"

When we are thankful for what we have, we thank God for the gifts He has given us. This verse teaches us exactly how we are to live a life of legacy that brings glory to God. We need to be grateful for all circumstances, not just the blessings God has given us. During one of my visits with a friend who was receiving hospice care because of a terminal illness, he told me he was both sad and glad about his diagnosis. During the final stage of his illness, it was hard for him to say all the things he wanted to say so he was unable to explain his reasons. But now in reflection, I think of him and think of his words which model what giving thanks in all circumstances means. This devastating diagnosis changed the last years of his life. He didn't get to enjoy his retirement years the way he thought he would. He had every right to be sad about his circumstances. Being glad despite a terrible diagnosis is exactly what giving thanks in all circumstances looks like. We face challenging circumstances related to our health, faith, finances, and relationships. Despite these challenges and circumstances, we still give thanks. When we give thanks in all circumstances our legacy love letters help our loved ones do the same.

Unstoppable Love Rejects Every Kind Of Evil

1 Thessalonians 5:22 reminds us, "Reject every kind of evil" (NIV). These are encouraging words our loved ones need to hear. When we encourage them and remind them to "Reject every kind of evil," they avoid giving evil a foothold, especially during seasons of grief. Evil sometimes can be nonaction or unfulfillment, a failure to fulfill God's purpose for your life and legacy. Our loved ones need encouragement to continue in their faith and to fulfill God's plan for their lives. An example of a legacy love letter which encourages a loved one to fulfill God's plan for their lives was captured in the movie *I Still Believe,*[82] which tells the story of Jeremy Camp. Jeremy Camp is a successful Christian musician who wrote a song and a memoir about his first wife Melissa who died of cancer shortly after their wedding. My favorite scene in the 2020 movie captures how his late wife expressed love and encouragement to him in a love letter. During his deep pain and grief, he smashes his guitar and finds a letter. The legacy love letter he received is shared in the movie. His late wife wrote, "So do one thing for me for my sake and for the sake of your gift … When you're

82 *I Still Believe.* Directed by Andrew and Jon Erwin, performances by K.J. Apa and Britt Robertson, Lionsgate, 2020.

ready, pick up your guitar."[83] She knew in his grief he would not be able to play his guitar. Her final words encouraged him to play again. I can't imagine the world without Jeremy's music. God designed him with the gift of music to share God's love with the world. His music has impacted so many lives. In Jeremy's case it was understandable that he was grieving his wife. Nobody would have faulted him for giving up music. But his story and song remind us that the God we serve is unstoppable and He wants us to keep going. Melissa's legacy gift of love and encouragement helped her grieving husband keep his faith and to teach others to still believe in God's faithfulness, truth and holy word.

Unstoppable Love Is Blameless

Use encouraging words to help your loved ones remember the Christian life is to be lived not in our own strength but through God's power and with God's blessings. Your letter of encouragement will encourage your loved ones to count on God's constant help despite the challenging circumstances they are facing. 1 Thessalonians 5:23 says, "May God himself, the God of peace, sanctify you through and through. May your whole spirit, soul and body be kept blameless at the coming of our Lord Jesus Christ" (NIV).

Unstoppable Love Endures

There is a prize for finishing the race. Philippians 3:14 tells us, "I press on to reach the end of the race and receive the heavenly prize for which God, through Christ Jesus, is calling us" (NLT). Your final words of encouragement help your loved ones press on so they can receive the heavenly prize. Unstoppable love endures through every circumstance as your loved ones press on to reach the end of the race and receive the reward of life—seeing God face to face and being reunited with loved ones.

83 *I Still Believe*, 2020.

Unstoppable Love Speaks The Word Of God

When you encourage your loved ones to continue going in the right direction, they will turn toward God. By faithfully speaking the Word of God to your loved ones, you can speak to who they are and who God has called them to be. You can speak into their character and their identity in Christ. Our words can hurt or heal, build up or tear down, bring joy or pain, and bless or curse. Pray and ask God to help you choose your final words carefully so your loved ones will be encouraged and become unstoppable.

Ephesians 4:29 directs us, "Do not let any unwholesome talk come out of your mouths, but only what is helpful for building others up according to their needs, that it may benefit those who listen" (NIV). Unwholesome talk does not build others up. Wholesome talk builds others up and helps them press on to finish the race God designed specifically for them. Your encouraging final words will help your loved ones remember God is going to accomplish through them all He has called them to do. Your wholesome talk benefits them as they press on with the belief they can be who God created them to be. Grandma Lindsey reminded her grandchildren, "***Always remember, "Life is what you make it!***" Grandma Lindsey's legacy encourages her grandchildren by building them up. She also gave them action steps to help them by telling them what to do each day: 1. Keep trying. 2. Keep praying. 3. Stay positive. 4. Be awesome – (Be your best self). 5. Become better – not better than anyone else, but better than the person you were yesterday. To read her legacy love letter see **Appendix Sample Letters**.

Scripture Prompt: "Study More!"

> "Therefore encourage one another and build each other up, just as in fact you are doing." – 1 Thessalonians 5:11 (NIV)

Prayer Prompt: "Pray Now!"

Dear Lord,

Your Word has shown us examples of how to encourage others by appreciating a quality, rejoicing always, praying continually, and giving thanks in all circumstances. Help us obey your commands so our final words are life-giving words that build character in our loved ones. Thank you for allowing us to encourage and help them maximize their potential as they continue to run the race you have set out for them. May our final words express encouragement and help out loved ones become unstoppable.

Amen

Writing Prompt: "Write Now!"

Journal and reflect about a time in your life a coach or a mentor helped you maximize your potential by expressing encouragement and life-giving words which built character in you. In 1 Thessalonians 5:11-23 (NIV), Paul gives many specific examples of how to encourage others: appreciate a quality, rejoice always, pray continually, and give thanks in all circumstances. Write about your loved ones and how you can express encouragement to them. Think about the qualities God created in your loved ones and the milestones you celebrated with them with joy and a cheerful heart. Continue to pray for them for their relationships, finances, and careers so they succeed in being who God has called them to be. Your legacy love letter and your prayers will encourage them despite the obstacles they have to face.

Worship Prompt: "Listen Now!"

"Unstoppable God" by Elevation Worship[84]

This song encourages our minds and hearts as we are reminded God's glory goes on and on. We have faith in a God who is unstoppable, and we

84 Elevation Worship. "Unstoppable God." *Wake Up the Wonder*. Written by Steven Furtick, Chris Brown, and Wade Joye. Provident Label Group LLC, 2014, https://www.elevationworship.com/.

are reminded nothing is impossible for God. This worship song reminds us we want our loved ones to be encouraged with the undeniable biblical truth that our God is unstoppable. We want our loved ones to know nothing is impossible for God. When our minds and hearts are filled with this biblical truth, we too become unstoppable, and nothing can stop us as we seek to express our love to the people in our lives who matter most. We become unstoppable as we rejoice always, pray continually, and give thanks in all circumstances. Our encouraging life-giving words will build character in our loved ones and bring glory to God.

Chapter Thirteen

T—Thankful: Express Gratitude

You will leave a legacy gift of gratitude that glorifies God when you speak Truth in love with faith and confidence. God's plans for your life and His purpose for your legacy is to express love and demonstrate His love in words and actions as you express gratitude to your loved ones by being *T—Thankful.* When you write a legacy love letter with a thankful heart, your letter expresses gratitude to God for the people He has placed in your life. The minute you put pen to paper and start listing what you are grateful for, you see your relationships in a different light and your relationships are strengthened. Recognizing you fulfilled your role in these important relationships God created you for, you see your life had meaning and a purpose.

A Grateful Mindset

A grateful mindset begins with a prayerful, heartfelt thank you to our Heavenly Father for showing His great love for us by sending His Son to die for us while we were still sinners. Romans 5:8 reminds us of God's great love for us and His gift of grace and salvation: "But God demonstrates his own love for us in this: While we were still sinners, Christ died for us" (NIV). As gratitude fills your mind and heart, you gain a grateful mindset because God's infinite love sets you free with the undeniable truth you are not the mistakes you make or the worst moments of your life because Christ died for you. Empowered by this truth, you have a grateful mindset and see your life and your loved ones differently. We are all the recipients of God's unmerited, unconditional love and His gracious gift of life. As recipients of this gracious gift of life, we express our gratitude with thanksgiving out of love and respect for God.

A Thankful Heart

A thankful heart expresses gratitude to God with thanksgiving. Psalm 100 shows us how.

Be Thankful

A psalm of thanksgiving.

Let the whole earth shout triumphantly to the Lord!
Serve the Lord with gladness;
come before him with joyful songs.
Acknowledge that the Lord is God.
He made us, and we are his—
his people, the sheep of his pasture.
Enter his gates with thanksgiving
and his courts with praise.
Give thanks to him and bless his name.
For the Lord is good, and his faithful love endures
forever;
his faithfulness, through all generations. (CSB)

This psalm of thanksgiving shows us how to give thanks to God by expressing our love with gratitude. We acknowledge that the Lord is God and we thank Him for His creation. We submit to His power and control over it. When we worship Him with praise, we give thanks to God and bless His name. We express our gratitude by serving the Lord with gladness. We live a life of obedience by looking for every opportunity to humbly serve Him. Our thankful hearts bring glory to God.

Thanks With Everything

Expressing gratitude allows us to give thanks to God with all our hearts. Psalm 111:1 says, "Hallelujah! I will praise the Lord with all my heart in the assembly of the upright and in the congregation" (CSB). The Message translation reminds us "***all my heart***" means with everything I've got, "Hallelujah! I give thanks to God with everything I've got …" (Psalm 111:1, MSG, emphasis mine). This verse reminds us to express our gratitude to God with thanksgiving with all our hearts and everything we've got. As you put pen to paper to express gratitude to your loved ones, give thanks to God with all your heart and everything you've got for these important relationships.

Thanks For Everything

When we give thanks to God with everything we've got, we are giving thanks for everything. Writing legacy letters allows us to express gratitude to God for everything including time spent with our loved ones, for life lessons, and for cherished memories. Legacy planning encourages people to review and give thanks for their history, values, memories, wishes and wisdom. When looking at values, estate planners are encouraged to talk to their clients about family legacy, which is usually defined by asking the question, "What do you want to be remembered for?" This is more important than historical information that provides details about the client's occupation or work history; church or fraternal organization memberships, and details about married life. By reviewing this important history it reveals gratitude for these experiences and identifies opportunities to make charitable gifts to colleges, organizations and churches. To look at values, estate planners ask, "What are the most important values in your life?" By identifying values it reveals their desire to provide for their loved ones and identifies opportunities to make gifts for the purpose of education or to preserve a family property. When attempting to capture life lessons to be shared, the question is, "What advice would you give your family?" Clyde wrote, "***When you receive the insurance money don't let them sell you an annuity or anything else for a year***." This is an example of a life lesson he wanted to share with his loved ones. To read his legacy love letter see **Appendix Sample Letters**.

Planning a legacy requires outlining personal wishes for family members to lessen the burden of making decisions about cremation and burial arrangements as well as personal wishes for a memorial or funeral service. These personal wishes include but are not limited to the type of ceremony; the choice of minister/pastor; a selection of a favorite Bible verse or literary quote; music selections; and even floral requests. When you give thanks *for* everything, you will know your values and what you want to be remembered for. As you plan your legacy with gratitude, God will change your heart for legacy and help you identify the life lessons, the cherished memories, and the personal wishes to be shared with your loved ones.

The Posture Of Thanks

Adopting the posture of thanks looks like the posture of humility because gratitude knocks us out and lays us flat. Author Erin Davis explains a posture of thanks by focusing on 2 Chronicles 6:12-14 which is Solomon's Prayer:

> Then Solomon stood before the altar of the Lord in front of the entire congregation of Israel and spread out his hands. For Solomon had made a bronze platform 7½ feet long, 7½ feet wide, and 4½ feet high and put it in the court. He stood on it, knelt down in front of the entire congregation of Israel, and spread out his hands toward heaven. He said:
>
> Lord God of Israel,
>
> there is no God like you
>
> in heaven or on earth,

who keeps his gracious covenant

with your servants who walk before you

with all their heart. (CSB)

Erin Davis helps us understand the posture of thanks by showing us gratitude will knock us out and lay us flat. She uses Solomon's posture of thanks as an example: "Here in 2 Chronicles 6, Solomon's body seemed electrified with thanks. First, he stood and spread out his hands, gratefully receiving the gifts of God's favor (v.12). Next, he knelt, lifting his hands toward heaven. We might expect Solomon to parade or puff up at this important occasion. Instead, he lowered his body into a posture of humility (v.13). Gratitude will do that; it knocks us out and lays us flat."[85] By focusing on Solomon's posture of thanks we learn what is required of us to express full gratitude for all of God's gifts. When we stand and receive the gifts of God's favor we are acknowledging his enduring love for us. Gratitude knocks us out and lays us flat as we humbly proclaim God's authority and faithfulness. Our words and actions reflect the psalm of thanksgiving as we serve the Lord with gladness, we acknowledge the Lord is God, and we praise and give thanks to Him for making us His.

The Posture Of Gratitude

Author Mark D. Roberts explains a posture of gratitude by focusing on Colossians 1:3-4, "In our prayers for you we always thank God, the Father of our Lord Jesus Christ, for we have heard of your faith in Christ Jesus and of the love that you have for all the saints" (NRSV). Roberts defines the posture as follows, "I think it suggests, not just persistence in thankful prayer, but also a posture of gratitude. I'm not speaking of a literal posture, but rather of a way of thinking, feeling, being, and acting. One who has a posture of gratitude sees all of life as full of God's good gifts. A person with this posture pays attention to how God showers us with blessings upon blessings. Spoken thanks to God flows naturally from such a posture."[86]

---

85 Davis, Erin. "The Posture of Thanksgiving." *She Reads Truth*, https://shereadstruth.com/the-posture-of-thanksgiving-2/.

86 Roberts, Mark D. "Living Fully, Living Gratefully: Developing a Posture of

To be like those who have developed postures of gratitude, Roberts suggests thanks will flow spontaneously and generously from your lips as gratefulness fills your heart because you pay attention to God's good gifts. Your legacy reflects your gratitude because of the way you thought, felt, and behaved. Roberts provides a prayer for a posture of gratitude, "Gracious God, thank you for all the gifts you shower upon me. Thank you for the multitude of gifts I've received even this very day. You are so good to me! Help me, Lord, to be thankful, not just every now and then, but persistently. May I live my life with a posture of gratitude. In what I think and feel, in what I do and say, in how I perceive and believe, may I be full of thanks. Amen."[87]

When you follow Robert's advice and ask God for guidance to live your life with a posture of gratitude, you will learn to be thankful in what you think and feel, in what you do and say, in how you perceive and believe. You will be full of thanks because gratitude turns everything you have into enough. You have counted your blessings, and you are thankful for each and every one. Your legacy love letter will reflect your posture of gratitude as gratefulness fills your heart and your thanks flows from your lips. You can write, "God has been so good to me! I thank God for the gifts he showers upon me everyday but you were the best one." Diane's husband wrote, "***You are the gift that I was fortunate enough to have received for what was in my heart. You are the proof that if one tries to live a good life and, even though there may be missteps along the way, that we all receive our just rewards. I was fortunate to have received mine while I was still on earth.***" To read his letter, see **Appendix Sample Letters**.

Set Your Hearts And Minds

As you write your legacy love letters, your heart will be filled with gratitude and thanksgiving. Upon reflection, you will give thanks to God for everything and count the blessings in your life by considering your faith, your relationships, your health, your work, and your hobbies. With

---

Gratitude." *Fuller De Pree Center*, 3 March 2020, https://depree.org/life-for-leaders/living-fully-living-gratefully-developing-a-posture-of-gratitude/.

87 Roberts.

a focus on gratitude, most people discover they have been overvaluing possessions and the pursuit of them while undervaluing time with loved ones. If this truth convicts you, it doesn't mean you are a bad person—Christian growth is a lifelong process. This is why we study God's Word to learn the rules for holy living and what Christians should do. The Bible even provides the antidote to materialism in Colossians 3:1 which includes the directive, "set your hearts on things above," followed by the directive in verse 2, which says, "Set your minds on things above, not on earthly things" (NIV). As we model this recommended behavior and set our hearts and minds on things above, we concentrate on the eternal. This is the antidote to materialism because it allows us to gain God's view of material goods which is the proper perspective in living the Christian life. This biblical truth helps us live here on earth seeking what God desires. As we set our hearts and minds on things above, not earthly things, we live in pursuit of a more meaningful life as we follow Christ and love and serve those around us and live each day for Christ. Our legacy will reflect a life well-lived and well-loved, not one measured by earthly possessions. In Luke 12:15 Jesus warns, "Beware! Guard against every kind of greed. Life is not measured by how much you own" (NLT).

Words Of Appreciation

A legacy gift of gratitude flows directly from your heart as you speak words of appreciation to your loved ones. In *Start with Your People*, Dixon provides ten exercises to help his readers put people first so they can develop the people-first lifestyle.[88] This book is a must-read to help you get started fully engaging in your relationships. One of the ten exercises is to *send thank-you notes* because people love to be thanked. Dixon explains, "They love to be recognized, and they love to help those who appreciate them."[89] His explanation is true both during your lifetime and after you are gone because your thank-you notes are legacy gifts of gratitude. The simple act of recognizing your loved one and appreciating them engages them fully in your relationship. Your written words of appreciation and your action of writing and delivering the note proves people in your life

88 Dixon, *Start With Your People: The Daily Decision that Changes Everything,* 207-222.

89 Dixon, *Start With Your People: The Daily Decision that Changes Everything,* 207, 210-212.

are the greatest assets you have because you have put them first. You are living a more meaningful life as you develop the people-first lifestyle and speak words of appreciation in everything you do.

Gifts Of Gratitude

Another exercise, Dixon teaches his readers to fully engage their relationships is to *express gratitude with a gift.*[90] He teaches, "We give gifts because we're truly appreciative. We simply want to express our gratitude. 'You mean a lot to me. I'm thankful for you. Here's something I thought you would enjoy.'"[91] Dixon's suggestion to express gratitude with a gift reminds me of Gary Chapman's five love languages because one of the love languages is receiving gifts.[92] As a marriage counselor, Chapman discovered the five love languages to best express affection to loved ones in the way they interpret as love. He explains visible symbols of love are important. He teaches notes and gifts are both physical effort and words of affirmation meant to express love. He says, "at the heart of love is the spirit of giving."[93] He explains gifts come in all sizes, colors, and shapes and can be expensive or free because they can be purchased, found, or made.[94] Your legacy love letter is a visible symbol of love which can be purchased or made. What is important is that you were thinking of your loved one. Gary teaches the thought expressed in actually securing the gift and giving it is an expression of love, "The gift itself is a symbol of that thought."[95] I pray God gives you a heart for legacy as He helps you express affection to your loved ones in the way they interpret as love so you can leave a legacy gift of gratitude. Your legacy love letter expresses your gratitude with a gift your loved one can hold in their hand and say, "Look, she was thinking of me," or, "He remembered me." You are leaving a visual symbol of your love and gratitude and your loved ones

---

90 Dixon, *Start With Your People: The Daily Decision that Changes Everything,* 207, 218-219.

91 Dixon, *Start With Your People: The Daily Decision that Changes Everything,* 219.

92 Chapman, 75.

93 Chapman, 83.

94 Chapman, 78.

95 Chapman, 77.

will feel loved. You have given your legacy gift of gratitude lovingly and well.

Life-Giving Words

"Speak life-giving words"[96] is another exercise Brian Dixon suggests to help his readers incorporate more life-giving words into their conversations. "Life-giving words inspire and encourage other people."[97] I highlight only three of Brian's ten exercises which help us show up each day to see and serve the people in our lives. I recommend this book and these exercises as you prepare to write your legacy love letters with a full heart of gratitude. As you develop the people-first lifestyle and the desire to invest in your loved ones, you will be remembered for making a difference and God's wondrous works will be remembered. Let your legacy be the investment you made in people because you speak words of appreciation, express gratitude, and speak life-giving words. Your legacy will reflect that your heart is set on things above, not earthly things. You will be remembered for your people-first lifestyle not your material poessessions.

Grateful Attitude

May God's peace rule in our hearts and cause us to have a grateful attitude. We are called to always be thankful which is an attitude of gratitude. Colossians 3:15 reminds us, "And let the peace that comes from Christ rule in your hearts. For as members of one body you are called to live in peace. And always be thankful" (NLT). The Message translation puts it another way: "Let the peace of Christ keep you in tune with each other, in step with each other. None of this going off and doing your own thing. And cultivate thankfulness. Let the Word of Christ—the Message—have the run of the house. Give it plenty of room in your lives. Instruct and direct one another using good common sense. And sing, sing your hearts out to God! Let every detail in your lives—words, actions, whatever—be done in the name of the Master, Jesus, thanking God the Father every step of the way" (Colossians 3:15-17, MSG). This verse reminds us to

96 Dixon, *Start With Your People: The Daily Decision that Changes Everything,* 207, 212-213.

97 Dixon, *Start With Your People: The Daily Decision that Changes Everything,* 212.

always be thankful. The best way to live with an attitude of gratitude is to cultivate thankfulness. You can live a legacy life by thanking God every step of the way and letting every detail in your life including words and actions be done in the name of Jesus. You are cultivating thankfulness by letting the Word of God rule in your heart as you fulfill God's plan for your life and purpose for your legacy. You will be remembered for your grateful attitude and how you lived with peace in your heart.

Start With A Simple Thank-You

When my children were young, I helped them write their thank-you notes for gifts by finding a preprinted card. There was no need to make the letter writing complicated. Once completed, this simple note card still counted as a thank you note. It was an opportunity for them to express gratitude for the gift they had received from a friend or family member. They were able to express their gratitude by filling in the blanks, it didn't matter if the thank-you note was preprinted.

Dear ____,

Thank you for __________.

Love, _____.

Remember this sample thank-you note structure when you are struggling with getting started. If you are faced with a blank page and you don't know how to begin your letter, begin simply by thanking your loved one for something they have done for you or a special memory. This statement of gratitude will fill your heart with thankfulness and your letter will express gratitude to God for the people he has placed in your life.

Scripture Prompt: "Study More!"

"And let the peace that comes from Christ rule in your hearts. For as members of one body you are called to live in peace. And always be thankful." —Colossians 3:15 (NLT)

Prayer Prompt: "Pray Now!"

Dear Lord,

We are grateful for all the blessings you have given each one of us, including your plans for our lives and your purpose for our legacies. You have called us to live in peace and always be thankful. We know we will run out of time expressing our gratitude, but we will not stop praising you and thanking you. We want to be remembered for our posture of gratitude. Help us express our gratitude to our loved ones so our legacy gifts of gratitude have an everlasting impact. Help us live our lives full of thanks in what we think and feel, in what we do and say, and how we perceive and believe. We dedicate the time we have left to set our minds on things above, not on earthly things.

Amen

Writing Prompt: "Write Now!"

Journal and reflect about God's blessings and all He has done in your life. Write about your posture of gratitude and humility. Think about what impact your legacy gift of gratitude will have on your loved ones. Consider what steps you can take so your legacy will be the investment you made in people because you speak words of appreciation, express gratitude, and speak life-giving words.

Worship Prompt: "Listen Now!"

"Counting My Blessings" by Seph Schlueter[98]

The lyrics of this song demonstrate a posture of gratitude: how to count our infinite blessings and thank God for all He has done in our lives. We are reminded of the brevity of life as we sing along to worship our God and acknowledge we will run out of time on this side of Heaven thanking God for all He has done in our lives. This worship song demonstrates how we can sing our hearts out to God and always be

98 Schlueter, Seph. "Counting My Blessings." *Counting My Blessings*. Written by Seph Schlueter, Jonathan Gamble, and Jordan Sapp. Provident Music Group, 2024, https://www.sephschlueter.com/.

thankful. When we acknowledge God's infinite blessings we see all of life as full of God's good gifts and we live our lives with a posture of gratitude and humility.

Chapter Fourteen

H—Hope: Express Hope and Sympathy

You will leave a legacy gift that glorifies God when you speak Truth in love with faith and confidence. God's plan for your life and His purpose for your legacy is to express and demonstrate His love in words and actions as you *H—Hope: Express Hope* and *Sympathy.* When we leave a legacy gift of hope and sympathy for our loved ones, our final words are not only sweet to their soul but bring healing to their minds and hearts. Proverbs 16:24 tells us, "Gracious words are a honeycomb, sweet to the soul and healing to the bones" (NIV). Your gracious and hope-filled words are not expected but are desperately needed by your loved ones. Your expressions of hope and sympathy provide healing to your loved ones' grieving minds and hearts. As you express your love to them with hope and sympathy, your final words lead your loved ones toward God and out of the valley of darkness of pain and suffering. You are leading them through their grief journey so they can find refuge and strength in God. They can come back to God seeking restoration and find His grace and mercy once again.

Eternal Hope

A legacy love letter with hope delivers a gift of eternal hope for those you leave behind since you reminded your loved ones you will be reunited with them in Heaven. When you write a legacy love letter, your loved one will receive a final goodbye. Your legacy gift of hope will have an impact on them. Your letter gives them the hope they need during their grief journey, the hope that they can only find in Jesus Christ. It is eternal hope that will allow your loved ones to look ahead with confidence and courage. Their hearts still ache but they will cling to the biblical truth that earthly separation is only temporary until we are reunited in Heaven. Since our loved ones will still grieve and experience loss, this eternal hope of Heaven provides them with the guiding light they need in the darkness of grief and despair.

Sympathy Is Kindness

Sympathy is kindness and support to our loved ones during their time of grief. Condolences or sympathy notes are intensely personal and emotional. When you express your love with words of sympathy, you are speaking understanding and compassion directly to their grieving hearts. As Christians we are called to have sympathy and to be responsive to the needs of others. Your words could mean the difference between continued pain and the road to healing. 1 Peter 3:8 reminds us to be sympathetic, "Finally, all of you, be like-minded, be sympathetic, love one another, be compassionate and humble" (NIV). Being sympathetic is just one of the five key qualities listed in this verse. We are called to live in harmony, which is being like-minded and pursuing the same goals. We are directed to love one another. We must have compassion as we show affection with care and sensitivity. And most importantly, we must be humble if we want to serve God effectively. When we are humble, we express our humility when we are willing to encourage one another and rejoice in each other's successes. By possessing these qualities, we will bring glory to God because our actions and behaviors are evidence of God's truth. When our legacy stories bear witness to a life of harmony, sympathy, compassion, love, and humility, our lives speak truth loudly and clearly. When our lives speak the truth, our pride becomes humility, and our insensitivity gives way to genuine love and affection for others. The purpose of our legacy is to show our loved ones our hope in Jesus. When our loved ones see Jesus in us, they see what Jesus has done in our own lives, which brings glory to God. When we embrace humility, we no longer view ourselves as more significant than others. Philippians 2:3 reminds us, "Do nothing from selfish ambition or conceit, but in humility count others more significant than yourselves" (ESV). When we consider others more significant than ourselves, we love them selflessly. This behavior exemplifies our faith since our culture encourages us to prioritize ourselves above all else and adopt a self-centered mindset. Jesus teaches us how to love selflessly because He humbled Himself to serve, heal, and ultimately lay down His life for us.

Prayers For Healing

As you write your legacy love letters, continue to pray for your loved ones and ask God to heal their broken hearts. Your legacy letter can be a prayer for your loved ones. Simply write, "I am praying for you now and I know God will answer my prayers here on earth even when I'm gone." When your letters offer kindness and support and prayers for healing, your loved ones turn toward God and allow Him to fight for them when the loss they are experiencing makes them unable to fight. As they turn toward God during their pain and suffering, they will find and know the treasure of His comfort. The treasure of God's comfort is a heavenly treasure that will belong to your loved ones. It is a legacy gift they can enjoy and an inheritance they will pass on to their loved ones. As they pray prayers of healing over their loved ones, they too will glorify God with their legacies as His wondrous works are remembered.

Gentle And Affirming Words

To live fully for God and bring Him glory, we must love mercy and act justly by providing kindness and support to our loved ones. Through our kindness, our gentle and affirming words have the power to instill hope and encourage our loved ones. When we comfort each other, we give each other strength. This legacy gift is a single act of kindness and support which has the potential to transform their entire life by bringing them out of the pit of despair and into a life of freedom. We live in a desperate and chaotic world, so this priceless gift of a legacy letter which offers gentle and affirming words can be the one thing your loved one needs to get through the day. When they can get through the day, they can get through the week. When they get through the week, they can get through the year. When they get through the year, they can reach higher ground and continue on the path of light and life that God designed specifically for them. Your legacy gift leads your loved ones back to the plans God has for their life and the purpose He has for their legacy.

Pour Out Their Heart With Tears – A Time To Mourn

When one grieves the loss of a loved one, they pour out their heart with tears. Psalm 6:6 says, "I am worn out from sobbing. All night I flood my bed with weeping, drenching it with my tears" (NLT). This verse describes what a time of mourning looks and feels like. During seasons of grief, we are sad and worn out from pouring out our hearts with tears.

God Blesses Those Who Mourn

God blesses and comforts us in our troubles. Matthew 5:4 promises, "God blesses those who mourn, for they will be comforted" (NLT). A pastor and a fellow hope*books author Mark Medley shines light on this biblical promise by explaining it might sound crazy that we are blessed when we mourn, but this is the only way to know the treasure of His comfort. Mark explains, "In our darkest time, He faces us, opens His arms to us, He welcomes us, and He fights for us when we are unable to fight."[99] You can remind your loved ones of this biblical promise. You can write, "Do not forget, God will comfort you in your darkest time and will fight for you when you are unable to fight."

---

99 Medley, 51.

There Is A Time For Everything

Just as we experience seasons throughout the year—winter, spring, summer and fall—there are seasons we experience as we live out each page of our legacy story. The Bible reminds us there is a time for everything, including a time to be born and a time to die. Ecclesiastes 3:1-8 says,

"There is a time for everything,
and a season for every activity under the heavens:

a time to be born and a time to die,
a time to plant and a time to uproot,
a time to kill and a time to heal,
a time to tear down and a time to build,
a time to weep and a time to laugh,
a time to mourn and a time to dance,
a time to scatter stones and a time to gather them,
a time to embrace and a time to refrain from embracing,
a time to search and a time to give up,
a time to keep and a time to throw away,
a time to tear and a time to mend,
a time to be silent and a time to speak,
a time to love and a time to hate,
a time for war and a time for peace. (NIV)

God's Faithfulness

We want our loved ones to know this biblical truth: God is faithful and He will be with them. Your legacy letters remind them of God's faithfulness as you express your love with words of sympathy. Sympathy cards are well-received by grieving hearts because our kind words offer love and compassion. Words of sympathy bring support to your loved ones at a critical time. Sympathy provides not only kindness but understanding.

Acknowledge Their Loss

It may feel impossible to find the right words to say but don't let this stop you from acknowledging their loss. As you acknowledge their loss, remember everyone deals with loss differently. Author H. Norman Wright reminds us, "Your grief experience is unique."[100] When you acknowledge their loss and offer your condolences, it can be enough to brighten their day no matter how they are experiencing or expressing their grief over their loss. You can brighten their day by writing, "I know this is painful and I am sorry I cannot be there with you at this difficult time." To provide loving words of sympathy, you can write, "I cannot imagine how difficult this must be for you." Your acknowledgement of their loss will bring them comfort and remind them they are not alone. Loved ones will grieve differently in expression, intensity, and time that is why H. Norman Wright reminds us, "You can't compare yourself with others and their grief."[101]

Losing A Spouse Or Partner

When expressing love with hope and sympathy to your spouse or partner, keep in mind losing a spouse or partner is devastating and destabilizing. In addition to the initial emotions of heartache, immense sadness, and grief, there are immediate and intense shifts in day-to-day life. Daily living looks completely different because the survivor no longer has their mate by their side. Not only are they facing life alone, but they also have to learn how to modify how they spend their time and money. They face the loss of their lifetime companion as well as a partner to contribute to both their health and well-being. Your final words remind them of the love you shared. Diane's husband wrote, "***I know that my love for you will carry you through the hard times and that in so many ways, you will feel my hand in yours***." To read his letter, see **Appendix Sample Letters**.

100 Wright, 17.

101 Wright, 69.

Loving Words Of Sympathy

When facing the sudden and unexpected loss of my dad, I received sympathy cards from family and friends. The cards brought me comfort during my season of grief as I read the words which reminded me I was not alone and the Lord would comfort me with His peace. Their loving words of sympathy reminded me I was not alone, "***No words can ease your loss, but I hope you find comfort knowing that you are in our thoughts.***" I was reminded that my family and friends were praying for me: ***"We wanted to let you know that thoughts and prayers are with you in your time of sorrow."*** And ***"Thinking of you. Words seem so inadequate, but may these help in some way to let you know that my thoughts are there with you today."*** I received loving words of hope and sympathy which brought me peace: "***In this difficult time, praying the Lord will comfort you with his peace, surround you with his love, and encourage you with his presence. So sorry for your loss.***"

Each heartfelt word served to bring me comfort so I did not believe the enemy's lie that I was alone. Their loving words of hope and sympathy demonstrated God's love in words and actions so I would be reminded of the truth that I was not alone. My circle of support demonstrated God's love in action by choosing to write and deliver the sympathy cards. As they expressed their loving, hope-filled words of sympathy for the sudden and unexpected loss of my dad, God's love filled my heart so I could continue to turn toward God for healing. Their kind words served to encourage me to seek refuge and strength in God and not in the world during my season of grief. As promised in Psalm 46:1 , "God is our refuge and strength, always ready to help in times of trouble" (NLT). Demonstrating God's love in words and actions did not have to end there. Feeling blessed with their love and kindness, I wanted to express my love and gratitude in return to those who reached out to me. Their kindness, support, and sympathy helped me keep my focus on God to find comfort and healing despite my grief. I found sympathy thank you cards with the sentiments: ***"Thank you for your kindness and support."*** And ***"Thank you for your kindness and sympathy."*** Both statements were correct because the cards expressed my love for them for their kindness in offering both sympathy and support when I needed it most. With a full heart of gratitude, I thank the individuals who blessed me with their sympathy and support during my season of grief. They allowed God to love me through them which showed His compassion. 2 Corinthians 1:3-4 says, "Praise be to the God and Father of our Lord Jesus Christ, the Father of compassion and the God of all comfort, who comforts us in all our troubles" (NIV).

Healing For Broken Hearts

We rely on God's help in times of pain and suffering. We can ask God to heal the sorrows of our loved ones' hearts as He begins to rebuild what has been broken or even destroyed. Psalm 147:3 promises, "He heals the brokenhearted and binds up their wounds" (NIV). Your final words remind your loved ones God is near, and God promises He will heal their broken hearts. The healing of their broken hearts will take time because they are going to miss us until they see us again in Heaven.

Grief Without Hope

My first published work was a piece titled "On Loss," which was featured in the *Mind and Eye Journal*, a publication by my junior high school. I was not a Christian then, so I did not know how to grieve with the hope of Heaven. I did not know the truth about God's victory over death, so I was stuck believing the lie death was the end of the story. I still read "On Loss" from time to time not because it was my first published work but because it reminds me what it was like to grieve without faith and the hope of Heaven. As I review the words expressing my feelings of loss during my adolescence, I am reminded of what it is like to be stuck in the place of darkness without God's truth and grace. I am also comforted now with the knowledge God was with me during my season of grief even though I did not know him personally yet. See **Appendix Sample Letters** to read "*On Loss.*"

Empathy And Sympathy

Author Brené Brown says, "Empathy is a tool of compassion. We can respond empathically only if we are willing to be present to someone's pain. If we're not willing to do that, it's not real empathy."[102] Brown distinguishes empathy from sympathy with these examples: "'I feel sorry for you' is an example of a person responding with sympathy. 'I get it, I feel with you, and I've been there' is an example of a person responding with empathy."[103] We are called to feel both empathy and sympathy for those who need help so we can serve God by supporting those in need. The Proverbs 31 woman is compassionate and generous because she shows a profound commitment to helping and serving others. Proverbs 31:20 says, "She opens her arms to the poor and extends her hands to the needy" (NIV). Your legacy love letter is a testament to the power of compassion. You are taking action to improve the lives of your loved ones with both empathy and sympathy. Your actions speak as loudly as your words as you feel empathy for your loved ones and take steps to alleviate their struggles. Your final words are a source of comfort and support which make a significant difference in the lives of those you love.

Jesus Is The Light Of The World

In the darkness we are lost; to find our way we need a guiding light. Jesus is ready to help us when we are lost, He is the light of the world. In John 8:12 Jesus promises, "I am the light of the world. Whoever follows me will never walk in darkness, but will have the light of life" (NIV). Looking for a light in the darkness is natural to us. We are accustomed to turning on our flashlights when we are outdoors after sunset; we turn on our headlights when we are driving in the dark; we light a candle at home when the power goes out. It's not because we are afraid of the dark, it is because we are created by our Heavenly Father to seek light as our refuge and strength in times of darkness. Our legacy letters help our loved ones find their way to Jesus, the light of life who can lead them out of the darkness.

102 Brown, Brené. *Atlas of the Heart: Mapping Meaningful Connection and the Language of Human Experience.* New York, Random House, 2021, 121.

103 Brown, 126.

God's Word Lights Our Path

Psalm 119:105 says, "Your word is a lamp for my feet, a light on my path" (NIV). This popular verse reminds us to let God lead us through life by keeping His Word close to our hearts. Our legacy letters provide hope and sympathy to our loved ones by reminding them God's Word is a guiding light which shows them the way. As we keep God's Word close to our hearts, He will show us how to leave a legacy gift that glorifies Him. Through His Word He guides our steps and provides hope to us so we can provide hope to our loved ones. Romans 15:4 says, "Such things were written in the Scriptures long ago to teach us. And the Scriptures give us hope and encouragement as we wait patiently for God's promises to be fulfilled" (NLT). As you bless your loved ones in a special way, your hope-filled words help them apply scripture so they can receive Godly wisdom. God's Word will light their way so they can stay on the right path as they wait patiently for God's promises to be fulfilled.

Serious Threats To Well-Being

I didn't understand the full meaning of the words anguish and despair until my dad died suddenly and I was processing my grief. For some reason, I needed to know what word identified the pain I was experiencing. I told a friend how I was feeling and she immediately recommended I read Brené Brown's book, *Atlas of the Heart.* Brené identifies the places we go when we're hurting: anguish, hopelessness, despair, sadness and grief. She explains hopelessness and despair are both emotions and experiences that can lead to feelings of desperation and can pose serious threats to our well-being.[104] I have included Brené's helpful descriptions here which distinguish despair and anguish to better understand the emotions and experiences that are serious threats to our well-being:

"Despair is a sense of hopelessness about a person's entire life and future. When extreme hopelessness seeps into all corners of our lives and combines with extreme sadness, we feel despair."[105]

---

104 Brown, 101.

105 Brown, 102.

"Anguish is an almost unbearable and traumatic swirl of shock, incredulity, grief, and powerlessness. Shock and incredulity can take our breath away, and grief and powerlessness often come for your hearts and minds. But anguish, the combination of these experiences, not only takes away our ability to breathe, feel and think—it comes for our bones. Anguish often causes us to physically crumple in on ourselves, literally bringing us to our knees or forcing us all the way to the ground. The element of powerlessness is what makes anguish traumatic. We are unable to change, reverse, or negotiate what has happened. And even in those situations where we can temporarily reroute anguish with to-do lists and tasks, it finds its way back to us."[106]

Brené's definitions of these emotions help us identify the threat to our well-being so we can confront it and ask God for help. Our legacy letters remind our loved ones God will set them free if they cry out to Him for help when they are in distress and anguish. Psalm 118:5 promises God answers us when we cry for help, "In my distress I prayed to the Lord, and the Lord answered me and set me free" (NLT). The difference between despair and anguish is that anguish is more than hopelessness because it literally brings people to their knees as they lose the ability to breathe, feel, and think.

Most people lose the ability to breathe, feel, and think but some people attempt to temporarily reroute anguish with to-do lists and tasks. Author H. Norman Wright describes this pain and denial by saying, "We are not immune to pain, but we resist its intrusion. There are several ways we use to do this. Some fight the pain through denial. We say, 'No, it isn't true' or attempt to live our lives as though nothing has happened."[107] Legacy letters give our loved ones something concrete to hold onto so they can cling to our hope-filled words which makes their anguish and despair less traumatic. Instead of living as though nothing has happened, and fighting the pain with denial they can fight the pain with God's help and He will set them free as He heals their hearts.

---

106 Brown, 91.

107 Wright, 9.

Anchor of Hope

Hebrews 6:19 promises, "We have this hope as an anchor for the soul, firm and secure" (NIV). Author Lee Strobel says, "That's because our hope is only as good as whatever we anchor it to."[108] He reminds his readers God loves us and is committed to helping us and by anchoring our hope to the One who has real power is the only way hope has any impact. Experiencing grief following the loss of a loved one can make us feel like we're stuck and unable to get on with life. That's why we want to give our loved ones practical guidance from God's Word about how to trust God during seasons of grief so they can anchor their hope to the One who has real power. Your legacy letter will anchor them in God's truth and grace and serve to help them with their grief. By reminding them how much God loves them and how much you love them, their hearts will be filled with God's love. When their hearts are filled with God's love, their broken hearts begin to heal because they have anchored their hope to the One who has real power and the strong desire to help.

But Take Heart!

But take heart! By trusting Jesus, we will be unshakable and assured, deeply at peace. In John 16:33, Jesus reminds us, "I have told you these things, so that in me you may have peace. In this world you will have trouble. But take heart! I have overcome the world" (NIV). When we take heart, we are deeply at peace because Jesus has overcome the world. This is not a shallow or temporary feeling, we are able to remain spiritually calm no matter what comes our way. This is good advice and words of encouragement from the bible. Tell yourself and your loved ones, "Don't lose heart!" or "Take Heart!" Then you will not grow weary or quit. Instead, you will press on to continue the race with a focus on truth and grace. Instead of being discouraged and overwhelmed, we let God's Word shape our thoughts, words, and actions.

---

108 Strobel, Lee. *The Case for Hope: Looking Ahead With Confidence and Courage.* Grand Rapids, Zondervan, 2015, 2022, 12.

Hope And Confidence

Hope comes from God. With hope comes an overriding confidence God is with us no matter what we face. Psalm 118:6 promises, "The Lord is with me; I will not be afraid. What can mere mortals do to me?" (NIV). When God is with us, we do not need to be afraid.

I agree with Strobel, who says, "How we face death tells us a lot about how we'll face life."[109] He explains this is because we do not need to be afraid of death. Instead, we live each day with the expectation God will fulfill His promises to us and He'll grant us eternal life. Strobel explains, "The Bible says that because followers of Christ have the hope of eternity, they can live their lives with boldness and strength."[110] This boldness and strength comes from God. It is this hope of eternity that changes the way we think about death. We know how the story ends so we can live with the confident hope God will fulfill His promises to us and our loved ones.

Strobel teaches us to base our hope on the One who has the power to truly change our lives and assure our eternity. He writes, "Biblical hope is the confident expectation that God is willing and able to fulfill the promises he has made to those who trust in Him."[111] When we trust God He will take us from a state of hopelessness about death to having real hope. We can remind our loved ones by writing, "Trust God and He will give you real hope" or "Trust God and He will assure your eternity."

Your hope-filled letters remind your loved ones that better days are ahead. Strobel says, "Hope is the inextinguishable flicker God ignites in our souls to keep us believing in the prevailing power of his light even when we are surrounded by utter darkness. It's the unswerving belief that better days are ahead, probably in this world and most certainly in the next."[112] Your loved ones can live their lives with boldness and strength despite their loss.

---

109 Strobel, 21.

110 Strobel, 21.

111 Strobel, 11.

112 Strobel, 2.

Letters Bring Joy

It is never too late to write legacy letters to a loved one, even if they have already passed away. Writing legacy letters to a deceased loved one provides a tangible reminder and an expression of what their lives have meant to you. My dad died suddenly and unexpectedly, which prevented him from expressing his final goodbye. Even though we lived miles apart, my children and I had seen him just weeks before at lunch celebrating his 83rd Birthday. None of us knew it would be his last. During my season of grieving my dad, I wrote to him even though he was already gone. For this special project, I chose a keepsake book of letters, *Inspired Letters to My Dad: Write Now. Read Later. Treasure Forever.* by Lea Redmond.[113] As I completed this book of twelve letters, the prompts helped me think about my dad and stories I wanted to share with my family in memory of him. This special keepsake book of letters contains helpful legacy prompts:

"A special memory I have of you is …"

"From you, I learned the importance of …"

"One thing I'm glad we share is …"

"I always think of you when …"

"I love that our family is …"

"One thing I admire about you is …"

"The best adventure we've had together was …"

"I've always wanted to tell you …"

"Thank you for …"

"In the future I hope we …"

The memories I was able to capture by remembering them and writing them down made me smile and find joy despite my season of grief. My dad's legacy will not fade from my mind. I will read these letters

113 Redmond, Lea. *Inspired Letters to My Dad: Write Now. Read Later. Treasure Forever.* Chronicle Books, 2016.

from time to time and cherish these memories and the love we shared. Even though my dad did not write his legacy letter with pen and paper, I was able to transcribe his legacy letter from the content of his life story and my memories of him. I agree with Pastor Aaron J. Anderson who says, "The way we choose to spend our time, the manner in which we treat our family and friends, and the personal character we develop and embody, these are the instruments of our life story."[114]

If you have lost a loved one who didn't leave a legacy letter or didn't have a chance to say their final goodbye, I hope you are encouraged by my story of how writing letters to my dad helped me find joy despite my season of grief. Reflecting on your deceased loved one's life story brings healing to a grieving heart and proves their life had purpose and meaning and brings comfort and encouragement for the days ahead.

Scripture Prompt: "Study More!"

> "Finally, all of you, be like-minded, be sympathetic, love one another, be compassionate and humble." —1 Peter 3:8 (NIV)

Prayer Prompt: "Pray Now!"

Dear Lord,

You bring us comfort when we are suffering. Thank you for helping us express hope and sympathy to our loved ones so they can find refuge in you. Our words are so inadequate but with your love they provide peace and comfort to our loved ones and their grieving hearts. Help our loved ones remember most of all we love them deeply. We pray their memories of our love bring them to a place of healing.

Amen

114 Anderson, Aaron J. "The Last Word Spoken About You." Blog post, 4 Oct. 2023.

Writing Prompt: "Write Now!"

Journal and reflect about God's supernatural powers and His ability to turn graves into gardens and mourning into dancing. If you have lost a loved one, spend time writing them a letter so God's wondrous works are remembered. Write your own letter by reflecting on the prompts I listed here or complete your own keepsake book for your loved one to contain your memories of them. *The Letters to My …* series by Chronicle Books includes a book for each family member: mom, dad, daughter, son, sister, and brother. Go to Chroniclebooks.com to find your keepsake book.

Worship Prompt: "Listen Now!"

"Graves Into Gardens" by Elevation Worship and guest Brandon Lake[115]

The song's title comes from a sermon by Pastor Steven Furtick, based on a passage from 2 Kings.[116] The lyrics remind us of the biblical truth that only God can turn graves into gardens and mourning into dancing. The song is meant to stir faith and remind people God's love and faithfulness endure. Songwriter Tiffany Hammer says, "There's moments we all experience in life where we find ourselves having a funeral for dreams that we once really believed in."[117] Her quote describes why this is a testimony song to the power and authority of our God. As we sing along, we sing our praises to a God who is better than anything here on earth, where earthly treasures fade and where man's praise leaves us empty. We are reminded God's mercy and grace finds us and fills us with His love, which satisfies all of our desires. We can confidently sing and declare this is our testimony: there is nothing better than God because He turns graves into gardens. We can look to Jesus as the truth and the light.

115 Elevation Worship and Brandon Lake. "Graves Into Gardens." *Graves into Gardens (Live)*. Written by Brandon Lake, Steven Furtick, Chris Brown, and Tiffany Hammer. Capitol Christian Music Group, 2020, https://www.elevationworship.com/.

116 Williams, Lindsay. "Elevation Worship's 'Graves Into Gardens' Testifies to the Resurrection Power of God." K-LOVE, 16 November 2020, https://www.klove.com/music/blog/music-news/elevation-worship-s-graves-into-gardens-testifies-to-the-resurrection-power-of-god-1029.

117 Williams.

Conclusion: Author's Final Words

Dear Readers,

I want to leave you with final words of encouragement before you set out to complete your legacy planning. The purpose of a book is to broaden perspectives by having an impact and leaving a legacy. As a hope*books author, I proudly invite you to visit the hope*books store in downtown Matthews, North Carolina. You will see the motto on the shop window, "To change your life, read a book. To change the world, write a book." My legacy how-to book may or may not change the world, but I hope it has changed your heart for legacy. Writing this book has definitely changed my perspective, it showed me God's plan for my life and purpose for my legacy. I set out to write an ordinary book about legacy, but I now know God's plan was greater. It was by God's design this ordinary book about legacy became an extraordinary book to encourage readers to embrace their legacy story and to glorify God by living fully in pursuit of a deeper faith and a more meaningful life. Thank you for letting me share the important message God wrote on my heart.

As you plan your legacy gift of love, faith, hope, and gratitude, take the time you need to complete this important task. Open your heart, mind, and soul to God's extraordinary plan for your life and purpose for your legacy story. Your acquaintances will know you for what you've done in your life, but your loved ones will always remember you for how you loved them. As you write legacy love letters, I pray your letter writing will strengthen your faith in God. When you draw closer to God, you learn the world's teachings are empty when compared with God's plan. God has shown us how to leave a lasting legacy, to love God and to love others. As you fulfill your obligation to be a faithful steward of the inheritance God entrusted to you, your reward will be peace of mind and heart.

One last thing before I go—I should answer the questions most people ask about legacy love letters. People ask where to place the letters once completed and if letters should be handwritten or typed. Clyde put his legacy love letter in his estate planning folder with his important legal documents so it could be found and read after his passing. Both Clyde and my husband's Aunt Sheryl typed their legacy letters—there is no requirement for legacy letters to be handwritten.

As I wrap up my letter to you, my beloved reader, my closing prayer is these words over you, "Let God's love change your heart for legacy so you live the legacy story God designed specifically for you and your loved ones grieve with eternal hope." My closing words of encouragement are to walk you through the steps of a vision exercise since you know the truth about legacy love letters bringing peace of mind and heart to both the giver and the recipient.

Please take the following steps:

Step 1—Imagine the legacy you could leave by writing your legacy letters to your loved ones;

Step 2—Picture your loved ones feeling loved and turning toward God for comfort and healing for their heavy and broken hearts during their time of grief;

Step 3—Envision the encouraging words you could share to help them through their grief journey; and

Step 4—Visualize the celebration which will take place in Heaven when you receive the reward of life—seeing God face to face and being reunited with your loved ones.

Now you have a heart for legacy and you can change your thinking and take action. The legacy mindset begins with you saying, "I will write a legacy love letter so *someday* my loved one will read it" instead of saying, "I will write a legacy love letter *someday*."

As your friend and legacy coach, I want to help you reach your legacy goals. Visit writelegacyloveletters.com or gwenchristeson.com for more help on designing your legacy gifts and follow me on social media for ongoing encouragement. You will have peace in both your mind and heart because your loved ones will receive from you a final goodbye and a final "I love you" to cherish. By planning your legacy, you are setting your loved ones up to be in a better position in the future, financially and spiritually. Not only are you leaving them peace of mind because you put your legal affairs in order, but you are also leaving them peace of heart with your legacy gift of love, faith, hope and gratitude. Your financial legacy honors God and provides for your loved ones. Your spiritual legacy invites them to join you in Heaven and reminds them of God's promises of eternal life.

Thank you for letting me walk beside you as God changed your heart for legacy. I pray God continues to bless you as you live each day in pursuit of a deeper faith and a more meaningful life. Instead of just saying you love people, your completed estate plan and your completed legacy love letters will be evidence that you *really* love them.

With love, your friend and legacy coach,

Gwen

Appendix Sample Letters

Clyde Hughes's letter and obituary

Eileen

If you are reading this it means that I went first. Two things I want to tell you.
When you receive the insurance money don't let them sell you an annuity or any thing else for a year. First enjoy what you might want to do.
The most important reason for this note is to tell you that I've had a wonderful life with you and I'm proud to have had you for my wife and lover.

I've always loved you and I will love you forever.
Clyde

Clyde Hughes

AUGUST 5, 1925 - FEBRUARY 21, 2014

Clyde Hughes, 88, of Pioneer, California, went home to be with his Lord and Savior on Friday, February 21, 2014. He was a husband, father, brother, son, grandfather and great-grandfather. He was the epitome of a gentleman, with the knowledge of Socrates. Clyde was a proud Army Air Corps WWII veteran who taught his children and grandchildren to be loyal, compassionate and selfless. Clyde showed love, kindness and discipline.

Clyde was born August 5, 1925 in Burbank, California, to Clyde and Myrtle Hughes. He was the youngest of 4 boys. Clyde grew up in Burbank and graduated from Burbank High School. He joined the Army Air Corps during World War II. Clyde owned a service station in Burbank for many years before working in the auto parts business. He was well-respected by all his clients and customers; known as a man of integrity.

Clyde married Eileen Hughes on March 16, 1947. They were married for 66 years. He left a beautiful love note for Eileen in the event he preceded her in death. He told her how proud he was to have had her as his wife, that he had always loved her and would love her forever.

Clyde loved his family and treasured time with his wife and children. They spent many summers at Bishop Creek. Clyde loved camping and fishing.

Clyde was very active at Sutter Creek Church of the Nazarene. He was the first person to walk up to someone new, shake hands and welcome them to church. He loved studying the Bible and preparing for his Sunday School class. Clyde came prepared with "just one question" and a gleam in his eye, ready to dig deeper into study of the Word. Everyone looked forward to Clyde's comments and questions and class now has a handout that is affectionately known as "Clyde's Corner."

Clyde was very involved with the Interfaith Food Bank. He and his wife Eileen have worked at the Food Bank every Wednesday for 14 years.

He is survived by his wife, Eileen Newton Hughes, and his daughters, Cheryl Ehlman and Kathleen Harmon. His son, Michael Hughes, preceded him in death April 8, 2008. Clyde is also survived by 4 grandchildren: Amy Brust, Keith Hohman, Adam Warren and Shannon Harmon; and 6 great-grandchildren: Frank, Nora, Jason, Emmalee, Cylus and Cassandra. He was looking forward to the birth of his next great-grandchild this summer. He was deeply loved and will be missed.

Honoring Clyde's wishes, there will be no memorial service. Donations in Clyde's memory can be made to the Interfaith Food Bank, 12181 Airport Road, Jackson, CA 95642.

Kathleen's dad wrote, "To my youngest of whom I am well pleased and proud. Do your best always and try to be outstanding in everything you do. Daddy"

Love letter from Anne Watson's mother dated 10-20-1990:

Dear Anne & John,

If anything has happened to us then please know that your Dad and I loved you both so very much. You will never be without that love no matter what you do. We are so proud of you both. I believe in God and Heaven and know that we, your parents, are in Glory and that the only suffering is what you do to yourselves. We will only know peace when you lift your heads up and go about your life – we will be together all too soon. Susan will be your greatest friend – go to her for advice. No matter what you do – do it the best you can. Outwork the competition! Remember there are many "downers" in life and not to put too much energy into any one of them. Believe it or not most of them will solve themselves. If you make some mistakes it's ok – everyone does.

Susan – please don't languish on this as you were "chosen" for this job. You have a very special family to help out

Make the most of your lives. Make happiness your daily goal. We'll be together soon—it is God's promise.   Love Mom and Dad

p.s. it is 7 years later 9-97 & I still stand by this message

Diane's letter from her late husband, Don Sanderson

"Hi Sweetheart-

If you are reading this something has happened to me and I wanted to have a chance to express my feelings about you and our life together. I know that you know that I love you … although I don't know if you have ever realized the depth of that love. I guess I have always dreamt that someday, someone would come into my life that would be all the things I ever thought I wanted. I have also wondered about the kind of person I am and if that counted in the scheme of life. Well, now I know … I must be a pretty decent person because God gave me you.

We have been together about ~~16~~ 24 years as of this date and aside from those things that I constantly gripe about, I have never been happier. You are truly my best friend, and if there is such a thing as a soul-mate, you are it. I love you so much that when I think of you, working in your garden or feeding your birds, tears come to my eyes. When I am away from you, I constantly think of you and what you mean to me. You are truly the love of my life.

Sweetheart, if God has taken me from you for some reason, I hope that you can remember me not for my crankiness, but for how much I loved you and for how much laughter and love you brought to me. You are the gift that I was fortunate enough to have received for what was in my heart. You are the proof that if one tries to live a good life and, even though there may be missteps along the way, that we all receive our just rewards. I was fortunate to have received mine while I was still on earth.

My Diane, please know that no matter what has happened to me, you were with me and your presence gave me strength because I know that someday, we will be together again. And as you live your life, I will be with you. I will always be looking over you, protecting you and giving you strength. I know that my love for you will carry you through the hard times and that in so many ways, you will feel my hand in yours.

Please remember our laughter and the wonderful things we shared. We will share them again someday.

I am here with Darren; Aunt Louise and those I love who have been taken. We are all waiting for you and watching over you.

I love you with all my heart,

Your Bubbie"

Ginna's Letter to Her Sons

Jeff and Jason 9/10/15

How does one write a note to their sons in case of their passing. I have no idea. All I know, is that through it all you two have been the best part of my life. You are good men and for that I am proud. I may not have always done the right things but I have always loved and treasured you both with all of my heart. Your children, Connor and Hannah are your gift to the world. Love them and help them when you are able. They are beautiful. Jeff, Ren is a very good woman .... I hope you two are together forever. Jason, Your wife is a special woman and deserves only the best. Please tell her I care about her and love her.

I love you both. I will see you in another place many years from now. I'll be chatting with my mom and we will know when you arrive.

Grandma (GG) Lindsey's Letter To Her Grandchildren

To My Grandchildren,

Ask yourself, "How and what do I want my life to be?"

Think about this, and then ask, "How do I make it that way?"

Everyone has a past, a present and a future to discover. We can't change the past, but we can plan on the future. We can make it unhappy and miserable by feeling sorry for ourselves or make it happy and wonderful by serving others, attending school, or working on a project that we enjoy.

If we will just try and if we will pray, our Heavenly Father will be with us and help us to do our best.

Always remember, **"Life is what you make it!"**

I will always love you, Grandma (GG) Lindsey

Things to do today:

1. Keep trying.
2. Keep praying.
3. Stay positive.
4. Be awesome – (Be your best self).
5. Become better – not better than anyone else, but better than the person you were yesterday.

Grace's letter

4/7/13

Dear Grace

It is with a heavy heart that I send my condolences on the passing of my dear & long time friend Ming. As you already know, we met back in 1956 when I was fortunate to have him as my roommate at Stanford. I still remember our first meeting. I had flown in from Hawaii & bussed to Palo Alto & then on to Stanford. I checked in the dorm & everything else was still closed. I was sitting on my bed wondering what to do when suddenly this guy walks in & announces, "Hi, I'm Ming Lai your roommate. Let's go out for lunch." He drove us to Palo Alto where we ate. He was the only person I ever knew that drove using his right foot on the gas pedal & his left foot on the brakes. In the afternoon, he talked me into going with him to the President's residence for his open house greetings for all new students. From that day on, everything was "uphill" for a great year with great memories thanks to Ming. I was one of the few people at Stanford that didn't have a car but with Ming, I didn't need one. On many weekends we went to San Francisco Chinatown for dim sum or in the evenings to attend socials with his friends from his U.C. Cal days. Once we drove to S. F. Chinatown early in the morning & took a "bus junket" to Tahoe getting back early the next morning (a little poorer). On another occasion he drove me to L.A. just so I could visit a family that had relocated from Hawaii.

After a while, the food in the dorm began to taste all the same so Ming brought his own shoyu from home. On many of his visits home on the weekends, he would come back with lop cheong &even though it was prohibited, he would cook rice & lop cheong in our room which obviously smelled up the dorm but we just kept our door & windows shut & ignored people trying to get our attention. It was such a special treat.

It was sad when it was time for me to go back to Hawaii but fortunately, we kept in touch throughout the years. . On my early vacations to CA, I always made arrangements to get together with Ming & on one of those trips, I got to meet you, Grace. On another occasion, he took me to visit a cousin that had come over from China that I had never met. Fortunately for me, when I found out that my cousin couldn't speak English & I couldn't speak Chinese Ming saved the day. Again it was sad when you folks had to relocate to Maryland. However, during our family trip to the East Coast, we visited you folks where you got to meet our 4 children. Even though he was very young, William still remembers, "Mr. Lai & his motorcycle." It was many years later when Terri was attending seminary in Massachusetts that on one of our visits, we drove down to visit you folks with Terri & Tami. .

I am so glad that eventually, you folks moved back to CA where we were able to get together from time to time & you folks could meet some of our grandchildren & was also able to attend Tami & Ed's wedding. I was always impressed that Ming remembered so many things about our Stanford days like how I used to sing, "Mule Train." It always brought back pleasant memories. Another high light was when you came to Hawaii with Amy, Ming's sister & your friends to take a cruise.

I thank the good lord for pairing us up at Stanford that day over 56 years ago. We used to joked to others that, "We're not friends, we're just roommates," when in reality we were both roommates & great friends.

During your period of grieving, our prayers are with you & your family, always & in all ways.

Wallace

Sheryl's letter

Sheryl was my husband's aunt who left a 40th Birthday card for him sixteen years before he turned 40 just in case she wasn't alive to deliver the card herself. She was still living and was able to deliver the card herself but it still had the original date of August 1, 1996.

The note on the envelope: "In case I'm no longer living on Erik's 40th birthday, please give this card to him. Love, Sheryl" The letter inside the card:

Dear Erik,

I know this is silly, but you know how I am so you'll understand. I saw this card the other day, and it was so exactly like you when you were young that I couldn't resist buying it just "a little bit early."

I hope I'm alive to wish you a happy 40th birthday, but if I'm not, I just wanted you to know …

how much joy you gave me when you were young,

how much pride I've had in you as a young adult, and

how much love I will always carry in my heart for you.

Happy 40th Birthday Erik! Love, Sheryl

My son Connor's Crayon Love Letter

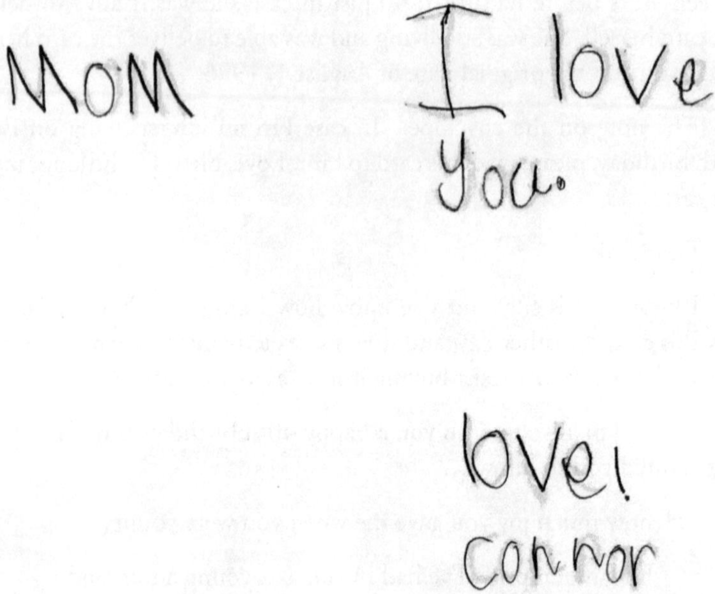

MOM I love you.

love!
Connor

Gwen (Thomason) Christeson's Alounence (Allowance) Letter

Not a legacy love letter but proof God created me to write letters.

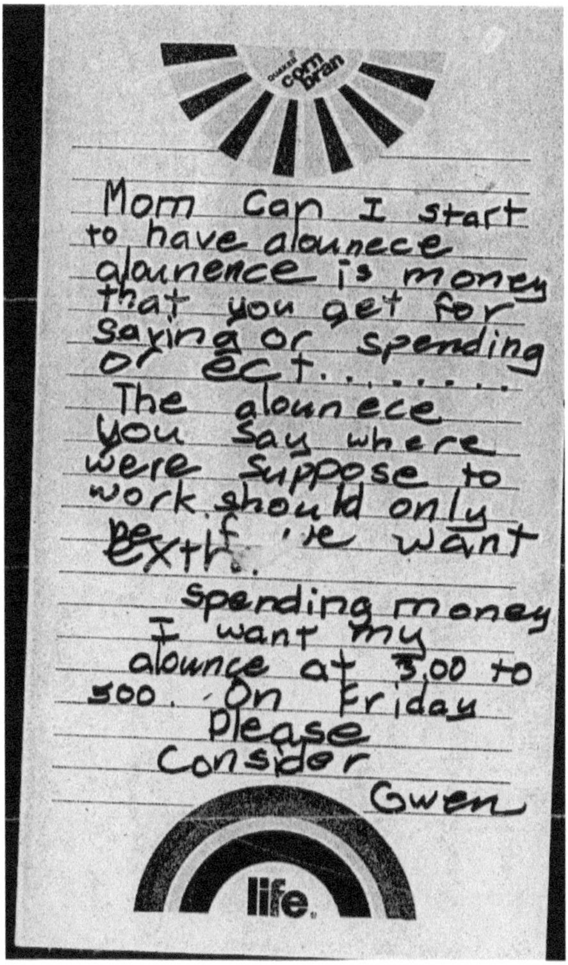

Mom Can I start
to have alounece
alounence is money
that you get for
saving or spending
or ect.......
The alounece
you say where
were suppose to
work should only
be if we want
extra
spending money
I want my
alounce at 3.00 to
500. On Friday
Please
Consider
Gwen

How Do I Love Thee?

My client Faye used this poem to help her write her love letter to her husband. She didn't know at the time that she was writing a legacy love letter.

"How Do I Love Thee? (Sonnet 43)" by Elizabeth Barrett Browning[118]

How do I love thee? Let me count the ways.
I love thee to the depth and breadth and height
My soul can reach, when feeling out of sight
For the ends of being and ideal grace.
I love thee to the level of every day's
Most quiet need, by sun and candle-light.
I love thee freely, as men strive for right.
I love thee purely, as they turn from praise.
I love thee with the passion put to use
In my old griefs, and with my childhood's faith.
I love thee with a love I seemed to lose
With my lost saints. I love thee with the breath,
Smiles, tears, of all my life; and, if God choose,
I shall but love thee better after death.

118 Browning.

Faye's letter to her Husband

Dear Leroy,

Elizabeth Barrett Browning wrote a poem that begins
How do I love thee? Let me count the ways ...
I am going to paraphrase her words for you and ask
Why do I love you? Let me list the reasons ...

- I love your funny sense of humor, that you can make me laugh, that you don't take things too seriously and can see humor in the absurd.
- I love that you never give up when presented with a problem. If you can't solve it one way, you will go at it from another perspective until you come up with a solution.
- I love that you don't hold grudges, even when hurt by another's insensitivity or mistaken judgment. You are willing to forgive, if not forget, an injustice.
- I love your sense of adventure, your willingness to explore new places and different ways of doing things. You do not think your way is the only way and are open to new ideas.
- I love your sense of direction, even though I do not understand when you say "this doesn't feel right." How does right feel to someone who could get lost in a paper bag?
- I love that you have never lost the wonder of being a child who believes in magic, that you are 80+ going on 6.
- I love your ability to take a raw piece of wood and create an object of beauty.
- I love that you never take yourself too seriously and can laugh at jokes about you.
- I love that you see the possibilities for excellence in others and have helped them realize their potential.
- I love that in this world of givers and takers, you are a giver par excellence!
- I love that while you asked me to marry you early in our courtship, you were willing to wait two years for my answer.
- I love that you took the shattered pieces of my life and helped me put them back together again. You have made me a better person than I would have been without you in my life.

Love you forever,
Sapphire

Karen's love letter song

Karen's Song

By Wyman Dickerson

If to Karen I should write a love song,
It would be about springtime and the trees.
The coast not far away, we could make it in a day
Enjoying sunsets by the sea.

I met her in the summer—it was hot then.
We had a love that wouldn't wait.
And before it was fall, we had said it all,
Love became our great escape.

Janis songs from long ago
In the hallway of time echo,
Reminding me when
Karen became the world to me.

On Loss

|Let me tell you about

the dreary days when the

clouds cover the sky and

the sun disappears and

the rain begins to fall forever.|

On Loss

by Gwendolyn Thomason

As it happens I am babysitting, and I am sick with a cold, and it is late. I have been sitting here thinking about Christmas time, and I have noticed that people's feelings are surfacing and they are caring for others' misfortunes, and that the memories of what I see and hear, what has been gained and lost, stay with me. All the memories are running right through me tonight, and I try to remember all that has been lost, because the quiet of the house and the loneliness of the night keeps filling me with emptiness.

I don't think there can be life without loss. I have heard that there is no gain without loss, and life, after all, is made up of experiences gained. But it disturbs me to realize that somewhere, some time, at the beginning, we began to lose. And even though we face this pattern every day, I still question whether or not we can live with it. Today the front page read: Pan Am Jet Crash Kills 273. And I heard on the radio some people discussing the pain the families of the dead must be feeling because of their great loss. Among the dead were American servicemen going home for Christmas and thirty-eight students from Syracuse University. And the feeling of loss spreads to all of us who picked up our papers this morning, saw the bold headline, and, feeling helpless, thought about the people we knew coming home for the holidays. It is this helplessness, this loss of power, that steals our security, just as we give helpless, silent approval to the deadliest government games: the building of nuclear weapons and the poisoning of the earth.

And now it is time to wonder about the things we have lost and what we still risk losing. I remember, as a child, being lost in department stores and other shadowy places. As the places slipped away and the shadows closed in, I remember wondering whether or not my mother had lost me or if I had lost myself. I remember losing precious items; in fact, I still lose them. And I know the feeling of great loss, the feeling that something is missing, a little piece of something dear, when someone I cared about, someone I needed, left me and moved to another city, and the illusion of their return lingered like a thick fog that I could see but could not grasp. Let me tell you of being left behind when my best friend moved to the other side of the continent, and I wrote letters and called almost every other week, and still I felt the loss of her friendship, because there were still so many things we needed to talk about and do together.

I know about the lost homework assignment; the teacher didn't believe that I was up all the night before. It is at times like these that I stop believing in myself, and I am lost. And when I begin to look for myself, it is like looking for an item in a lost-and-found box; it's filled with many lost articles, but mine is never there.

Let me tell you about the dreary days when the clouds cover the sky and the sun disappears and the rain begins to fall forever. Then is when the powerful feeling of misery surrounds me and soaks into my skin and reaches my heart. On some days I'll be strong and shrug it off my shoulders, and on other days it reaches my insides and I feel that something is missing, and I wonder what it could be, as if I hadn't guessed already. And there are the lonely days when the things around me remind me too easily of what has been lost. Right now I see a picture of the family in whose house I sit-the children are asleep upstairs. Their dog, Jackson, is in the picture, too. A couple months ago the dog ran out the front door and disappeared into the grey evening and didn't come back as he usually did. After he was gone for a few days, they posted "Lost Dog" signs on every conceivable telephone pole. One day a woman called; she had found the dog. It had been hit by a car. When Lynn and Fred held the phone and heard the news, the memories, the eight years of the dog's companionship, began to slip from their grasp, and they tried to fight the feeling of loss overpowering their hearts.

> |And now it is time to wonder about the things we have lost and what we still risk losing.|

I can tell you about losing to death. I remember when, in the seventh grade, our gym teacher died, and we attended his funeral. And there we were, standing in a room of misery, and all the memories of Coach Shig were floating around for anyone to hang on to, and his spirit was whispering in the ears of those who listened to the heartbeat. Let me tell you of walking up the aisle to the body, still and cold, and not believing it had happened, and feeling alone and lost even though my closest friends were with me. And let me tell you of the long drive home, trying not to lose him to the strong hold of death, yet all the time losing hold of the security of life.

And what have we gained from these losses? Tell me strength, but how, if we feel so weak. Tell me courage, but how, if we feel so defeated. Tell me experience, but how, if we wished it had never happened. Tell me there is hope and that someday we will find what we are looking for, because until then we are lost.[119]

119 Thomason (now Christeson), Gwendolyn. "On Loss." The Mind and Eye, vol. 2, June 1989, 108–109.

www.ingramcontent.com/pod-product-compliance
Lightning Source LLC
Chambersburg PA
CBHW031512120626
46545CB00005B/1842